SHAPE IT! 3

COMBO B

STUDENT'S BOOK

WITH DIGITAL PACK

Samantha Lewis and Daniel Vincent
with Andrew Reid

CAMBRIDGE UNIVERSITY PRESS

CB081702

CONTENTS

5 How can we save our planet?

LEARNING OUTCOMES

I can ...

- understand texts about saving our planet
- give an opinion in a discussion
- write an opinion essay
- understand how to use conditionals
- talk about planet Earth and natural environments
- use techniques to remember vocabulary and understand how I learn
- use reference words

Start It!

1 Look at the photo. Do you like it? Why?
2 Before you watch, which animals are in danger of dying out? Why?
3 Choose an animal from the video. What has happened to it? Watch and check.
4 What can we do to help these animals?

Watch video 5.1

p61

Grammar in Action 5.2

p63

Grammar in Action 5.3

p64

Everyday English 5.4

p66

Globetrotters 5.5

VOCABULARY

Planet Earth

5.01 **1** Match the words with the icons (1–12). Then listen, check, and repeat.

carbon dioxide	☐	pollution	☐
climate change	☐	solar power	☐
endangered species	☐	the environment	☐
energy	☐	the planet	☐
marine life	☐	waste	☐
oxygen	☐	wildlife	1

LEARN TO LEARN

Look, Cover, Remember

Use the look, cover, remember technique to help you learn new vocabulary.

2 Look at the words in Exercise 1 for one minute. Then close your book. Write the words you can remember. Compare with a partner.

3 Match the words from Exercise 1 with the verbs to make collocations.

produce: waste P

protect: wildlife S

reduce: pollution

destroy: the planet

4 Which of your collocations in Exercise 3 are problems and which are solutions? Write *P* (problems) or *S* (solutions) after the collocations.

Use It!

5 Tell your partner a problem from Exercise 3. Can they think of a solution?

Explore It!

Guess the correct answer.

We cut down … trees each day so that we can have toilet paper!

a 27,000 b 5,000 c 100,000

Find another interesting fact about planet Earth. Then write a question for your partner to answer.

READING

A News Story

1 **Look at the photos and the title of the news story. What problems do we have with our oceans?**

5.02 2 **Read the news story and check.**

3 **Complete the news story with the phrases.**

a giant floating islands of waste
b fish, sea birds, and other marine life eat them
~~c bags, bottles, and straws~~
d if we collect all the plastic
e the plastic from the ocean and recycle it
f it takes around 450 years for a plastic bottle to disappear

4 **What do these numbers in the news story refer to?**

1 22,000 species of fish in the ocean
2 5.25 trillion ______
3 five ______
4 2050 ______
5 16 ______
6 2.6 million ______

5 **Find words in the text (including the missing phrases) that mean ...**

1 movements of water. ______
2 thin pieces of plastic you drink through. ______
3 very big. ______, ______
4 objects that stop things or people from going somewhere. ______

Voice It!

6 **Discuss the questions.**

1 What do you think of Boyan's project?
2 What other problems could plastic in the ocean cause?
3 Can you think of any solutions?

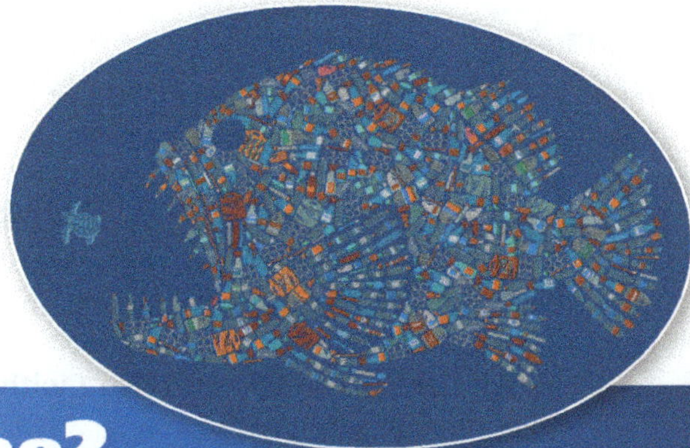

Can We Save Our Oceans?

Did you know there are over 22,000 species of fish and around two million whales in our oceans? However, something terrible is happening, and if it doesn't stop soon, it may destroy our oceans forever. Our oceans are filling up with plastic: [1] c . There are over 5.25 trillion pieces! The plastic moves from rivers into the ocean; then ocean currents push it together to make [2] ___ . There are five enormous areas of plastic pollution, called garbage patches. One in the Pacific Ocean is twice the size of France! The main problem is that the plastic takes an extremely long time to disappear. Did you know that [3] ___ ? Scientists predict that unless we do something to reduce the waste, by 2050 there could be more plastic in the ocean than fish. This is because the plastic breaks into smaller pieces and then [4] ___ and die.

But maybe Boyan Slat has the answer. When he was 16, he went on vacation to Greece and was shocked when he saw more plastic bags than fish in the ocean. Back in the Netherlands, Boyan started a school project to reduce ocean pollution and explained that [5] ___ , we might be able to protect our oceans. He shared his ideas on YouTube and got over 2.6 million views. In 2013 he started "The Ocean CleanUp," a program to collect [6] ___ . Long barriers float in the ocean and catch all the waste and then boats take it back to land to recycle it. Nobody is sure if Boyan's project will be successful, but we'll destroy our beautiful oceans if we don't do something now!

Finished? p122 Ex. 1

Watch video 5.2
How many species of sea turtles are in danger?
Why may people put signs up on the beach?

GRAMMAR IN ACTION

The First Conditional

If- Clause	Main Clause
If it **doesn't** [1] ___stop___ soon,	it **may** destroy our oceans forever.
Unless we [2] ________ something to reduce the waste,	by 2050 there **could** be more plastic in the ocean than fish.
[3] ________ we **collect** all the plastic,	we **might** be able to protect our oceans.
Main Clause	***If*- Clause**
We [4] ________ **destroy** our beautiful oceans	**if** we **don't do** something now.

Pronunciation p142

1 **Complete the examples in the chart above. Use the news story on page 60 to help you.**

2 **Match the sentence beginnings with the endings.**

1 If I have enough money,
2 Unless we meet before 8 p.m.,
3 Mario might not come to the party
4 They could lose the game next month
5 You will be cold

a if you don't wear a jacket.
b if they don't start training.
c we won't have time to buy tickets.
d if he doesn't finish work on time.
e I might go on vacation.

Get It Right!

We use **may**, **might**, and **could** when we are less sure of the result.
If I go to college, I might study biology, but I'm not sure.

3 **Put the words in the correct order to make sentences.**

1 we recycle / we might / our plastic, / If / reduce pollution
___If we recycle our plastic, we might reduce pollution.___

2 the planet / stop climate change, / If / we / won't get hotter and hotter
____

3 if we / We / collect plastic in the ocean / could reduce the enormous plastic garbage patches
____

4 unless we / Many animals / take care of our planet / will die
____

4 (5.05) **Complete the conversation with the correct form of the verbs in parentheses. Then listen and check.**

DJ Thank you for coming to tell us how we can help save our planet. What [1] ___will happen___ (happen) if climate change [2] ________ (not slow down)?

JEN Well, we know that the ice in the polar regions is melting, so if Arctic animals like polar bears [3] ________ (lose) their homes, they [4] ________ possibly ________ (die out).

DJ No polar bears? Oh, no!

JEN And unless we [5] ________ (stop) throwing away plastic, it is possible that a lot of marine life [6] ________ (disappear), too.

DJ That's very sad.

JEN Yes, but if we [7] ________ (not use) plastic bottles, we [8] ________ (help) reduce plastic waste. Unless we [9] ________ (reduce) pollution now, we [10] ________ (destroy) our beautiful planet for sure.

Use It!

5 **Complete the sentences about you. Then compare with a partner.**

1 If I have some free time this week, …
2 If I don't finish all my homework, …

Finished? p122 Ex. 2

VOCABULARY AND LISTENING

Natural Environments

5.06 **1 Match the words with the photos (1–10). Then listen, check, and repeat.**

bay	☐	iceberg	☐	volcano	☐
cave	☐	rainforest	☐	waterfall	☐
cliff	☐	stream	☐		
coast	1	valley	☐		

5.07 **2 Listen and write the places you hear from Exercise 1 in your notebook.**

1 waterfall

LEARN TO LEARN

Drawing Pictures

Drawing pictures of new words can help you remember them.

3 Work in small groups. Take turns drawing pictures of the words from Exercise 1. Who can guess the word first?

Use It!

4 Which words from Exercise 1 …

1 are near where you live?

2 have you visited?

A Class Discussion

5.08 **5 Listen to a class talking about ways to protect the environment and number the words in the order you hear them.**

blankets	☐	clouds	☐	sunglasses	1
caves	☐	showers	☐	worms	☐

5.08 **6 Copy the chart in your notebook. Listen again and complete the notes.**

Object(s)	Idea	How It Protects the Environment
sunglasses	Reflect the sun's rays away from the Earth.	reduces the Earth's temperature

Voice It!

7 Discuss the questions.

1 Which idea do you like the best? Why?

2 Which idea do you think is the craziest?

8 EXAM **Ask and answer the questions with a partner.**

Student A:

What natural environments is your country famous for?

Which natural environment would you like to see or explore?

Student B:

What is your favorite natural environment?

Which natural environment would you like to know more about?

Watch video 5.3
Which natural environment words does she mention? What transportation would people use if she ruled the world?

GRAMMAR IN ACTION

The Second Conditional

	If- Clause	Main Clause
+	[1] ________ we **lived** in caves,	we **would reduce** the energy we use.
	Main Clause	***If-* Clause**
–	We [2] ________ **use** so much water	**if** we **took** shorter showers.
?	What **would happen**	if we [3] ________ more clouds?
	[4] ________ we **reduce** waste Yes, we **would**. / No, we [5] ________.	if we **kept** worms in the kitchen?

1 **Complete the examples in the chart above.**

2 **Circle the correct words.**

1. If we *made* / *would make* houses from recycled materials, we *reduce* / *'d reduce* waste.
2. If we *would have* / *had* more electric cars, we *'d produce* / *produce* less carbon dioxide.
3. What *would happen* / *happened* if people *wouldn't use* / *didn't use* plastic bottles?

5.09 **3** **Complete the conversation with the correct form of the verbs. Then listen and check.**

be (x2)	can	~~do~~	drive	have
listen	not be	not have	work	

RITA So, what [1] __would__ you __do__ if you [2] ________ change anything in the world?

OSCAR Well, the first thing to go would be all exams and homework. Can you imagine how good school [3] ________ if we [4] ________ exams or homework?

RITA Ha ha! Great idea! Well, I'd make all cars electric. If we only [5] ________ electric cars, there [6] ________ so much pollution.

OSCAR Well, I'd give people more free time because if people [7] ________ more free time, they [8] ________ harder at school.

RITA Yeah, and I'd play music on the street. If we all [9] ________ to more music, we [10] ________ much happier.

4 **Write second conditional sentences.**

1. The Internet exists. I send messages to my friends and family all the time.
   If the Internet didn't exist, I wouldn't send messages to my friends and family all the time.
2. I go to school every day. I don't play a lot of video games. If I didn't ________
3. I get up early to go to school. I don't sleep for a long time. ________
4. I have a computer. I can watch movies and TV shows every day. ________

Use It!

5 **Put the words in the correct order to make questions. Then ask and answer with a partner.**

1. lived forever / the world be like / What would / if people / ? ________
2. How would / people could fly / if / life be different / ? ________
3. would happen / if we / memories / What / didn't have / ? ________
4. if you / What would / you do / were invisible / ? ________

Finished? p122 Ex. 3

SPEAKING

Giving Your Opinion

5.10 **1 Listen to the conversation. What do Josie and Marc think about zoos and marine parks?**

JOSIE I'm off to see my cousins. We're going to the park or the zoo, I think. Wanna join us?

MARC Well, if you go to the zoo, I'll have to pass. I don't like the idea of huge animals like elephants in small spaces. It's not cool.

JOSIE They have enough space. And don't forget that if we didn't have zoos, a lot of animals would disappear. They protect endangered species.

MARC Yes, maybe you're right, but have you ever thought about how the animals feel?

JOSIE Yeah, but remember that zoos take care of animals. And kids learn tons about them from visiting zoos.

MARC But marine parks aren't educational. They're just for entertainment. It would be much kinder to animals if we closed them!

JOSIE If we didn't have marine parks, some kids would never get to see animals such as dolphins or killer whales.

MARC I see your point, Josie, but let's agree to disagree.

2 Match the uses (1–3) with the phrases in the *Useful Language* box.

1 trying to get someone to change their opinion
2 showing you agree a little
3 showing you disagree

Useful Language

- Don't forget that … ☐
- I see your point, but … ☐
- Let's agree to disagree. ☐
- Maybe you're right, but … ☐
- Remember that … ☐

3 Match the uses (1–4) with the phrases in the *Everyday English* box.

When you …

1 want to invite someone somewhere
2 don't want to go somewhere with someone
3 are going somewhere
4 don't like something

Watch video 5.4
Everyday English

I'll have to pass.	☐	I'm off to …	☐
It's not cool.	☐	Wanna join us?	☐

PLAN

4 Do you agree or disagree with these ideas? Write notes.

1 We shouldn't keep wild animals as pets.
____

2 Plastic should be banned.
____

3 All transportation should be electric.
____

4 It's OK to cut down rainforests.
____

5 Work in pairs. Compare your opinions. Plan a conversation.

SPEAK

6 Practice a conversation. Remember to use the first and second conditional and phrases from the *Useful Language* and *Everyday English* boxes.

CHECK

7 Work with another pair. Listen to their conversation and decide what idea they are talking about. Do you agree with their opinions?

WRITING

An Opinion Essay

Who Should Protect the Planet?

1 ☐ Earth is a beautiful planet with amazing coasts, rainforests, and icebergs. However, we are not taking care of it, and unless we act now, we might destroy it forever. But who should protect our planet?

2 ☐ Some people believe that governments and big organizations should stop climate change. However, the planet belongs to everyone, and in my view, we should all reduce, reuse, and recycle. Did you know that people have made clothes, roads, and even houses from old plastic bottles? Furthermore, we should refuse to buy any more plastic bottles or bags.

3 ☐ In addition, we should use cleaner energy. For instance, if cars had solar panels, they would produce clean energy and reduce pollution.

4 ☐ In summary, in my opinion, if we all do small things to help every day, we will reduce climate change and protect our beautiful planet for the children of the future.

1 Read Camila's essay. Which of her ideas do you like? Why?

2 Match information a–d with paragraphs 1–4.

a her main idea and examples to support her opinion

b an introduction with a question for you to think about

c a conclusion to summarize her opinion

d a second idea to support her main opinion

3 Match the uses (1–4) with the words and phrases in the *Useful Language* box.

To introduce …

1 an opinion

2 a new idea

3 a conclusion

4 a contrast

Useful Language

Furthermore, … ☐
In addition, … ☐
In my view, … ☐
Some people believe that … ☐
However, … ☐
In my opinion, … ☐
In summary, … ☐

PLAN

4 Write your own opinion essay. Choose a topic. Think of two ideas to support your opinion. Write notes.

pollution and its effect on the environment
how to protect the planet

Idea 1 ______

Idea 2 ______

5 Decide what information to include in each paragraph. Use the information in Exercise 2 to help you.

WRITE

6 Write your opinion essay. Remember to include four paragraphs, the first and second conditional, and words and phrases from the *Useful Language* box.

CHECK

7 Do you …

- have an introduction with a question for the reader to think about?
- have ideas and examples to support your opinions?
- have a conclusion to summarize your opinion?

Finished? p122 Ex. 4

AROUND THE WORLD

Globetrotters
Watch video 5.5
Take Action Now!

- What is the problem in the Congo Basin?
- Which organization helps animals?
- How is the Mexican government helping?

READING

A Journal

1 Look at the photo and answer the questions.

1 Where do you think the person is?
2 What type of natural environment is it?
3 What is difficult about her lifestyle?

2 Read the journal and check. 5.11

3 Complete the spidergram.

Nenets and Their Reindeer

Where They Travel
The reindeer lead the Nenets to either the north or south of Siberia to look for food.

When They Travel
____

How Far They Travel
____

Houses
____

Clothes
____

Food and Drink
____

Wednesday, October 24 – Snowstorm!

Today we only walked a few kilometers because of the snowstorm. It's amazing how the reindeer know which direction to go in and don't get lost, even in a storm! The Nenets are **nomads** and follow the reindeer on their 1,000 km journey twice a year. In the summer they travel to the north of Siberia and in the winter to the forests in the south to look for food.

I don't think the Nenets would be able to survive without their reindeer. They provide them with everything: their clothes, their food, their tools, their transportation and even their houses. The Nenets use around 120 reindeer skins, or **hides**, to make each house, and they're so warm! Well, they have to be, I guess! If they didn't use reindeer hide for their clothes and houses, they wouldn't be able to survive when it's –50 °C.

We arrived here this evening and set up camp in the dark. My job was to build a wall of snow around the house to protect us from the **icy** wind. I asked why they travel when it's so cold and dark, and they said that they have to follow the reindeer. If they waited for warm weather and light, they wouldn't move for months. But every three days, they pack up and travel a few more kilometers.

We had dinner in the house around the fire. Raw reindeer meat mixed with reindeer blood and cheese from the reindeer milk. Surprisingly, it was delicious and very **nutritious**, too! The Nenets eat reindeer for every meal. They said that if it's warmer tomorrow, we'll have a picnic outside. By warmer, I think they mean –20 °C!

They tell me that the temperature is getting warmer because of climate change. This is making it more difficult for the reindeer to find enough food. And it also means that traveling is more dangerous. The Nenets walk across a giant frozen river. The river freezes later in the fall, and if it doesn't freeze completely, the ice could break. Unless we try to reduce climate change, it might be difficult one day for the Nenets and their reindeer to live as they have for thousands of years.

4 **Match the words in bold with the definitions.**

1 animal skins ________________

2 people who travel a lot and don't live in the same place for long ________________

3 extremely cold ________________

4 healthy, provides a lot of energy ________________

Voice It!

5 **Discuss the questions.**

1 Being resourceful means being good at finding solutions to problems. Why is this necessary for the Nenets?

2 What problems have the Nenets solved?

3 How can we be more resourceful with challenges in our own environment?

LEARN TO LEARN

Reference Words

We use reference words such as *it, they, its, their,* or *them* to avoid repeating the same noun.

6 **What do the words in bold mean? Look at the journal again to help you.**

a [1]**They** provide [2]**them** with everything; [3]**their** clothes, their food …

b And [4]**they**'re so warm! Well, they have to be, I guess.

c By warmer, I think [5]**they** mean −20 °C!

d If [6]**it** doesn't freeze completely, the ice could break.

1 reindeer

2 ________________

3 ________________

4 ________________

5 ________________

6 ________________

Explore It!

Guess the correct answer.

Nenets *use / don't use* cell phones.

Find another interesting fact about the Nenets. Then write a question for your partner to answer.

SHAPE IT!

CULTURE PROJECT

A Magazine Article

A magazine article gives interesting and detailed information about a topic. In groups, prepare a magazine article about a tribal nation.

NO FOOD FOR OUR REINDE

The Nenets live in Siberia. It's very cold! They are nomads and do a 1,000 km journey twice a year with their reindeer to look for food.

Life in Siberia can be difficult. The Nenets depend on their reindeer to survive. The reindeer provide them with everything: food, clothes, transportation and accommodation.

The Nenets have lived in the Siberian Arctic for over a thousand years, but their way of life is at risk because of climate change. They now face serious problems. melting. This means that the Nenets and their reindeer have to wait longer to be able to travel. If there was enough ice on the lakes, they would be able to travel easily and find food in new places. Some of the lakes in Siberia have already disappeared because of changes in the weather. This means and more difficult to find food. If the lakes disappe the Nenets won't be able to find any fish. Climate change has also led to other problems: hungry polar bears have started to enter their camps in search of food. They are a danger to both peopl and reindeer. If they ha

Teacher's Resource Bank

5 REVIEW

VOCABULARY

1 Circle the noun that we can't use with each verb.

1 **produce:**
energy carbon dioxide
solar power endangered species

2 **protect:**
wildlife oxygen marine life
the environment

3 **reduce:**
waste climate change the planet
carbon dioxide

2 Circle six natural environments in the wordsnake.

eathbayartcliffforteicebergfulrainforestionvolcanostwaterfallennew

GRAMMAR IN ACTION

3 Circle the correct words.

[1]*If / Unless* you take your own bottle to London's Natural History Museum, you [2]*don't / won't* see plastic water bottles there. If visitors [3]*want / might want* to drink water at the museum, they [4]*will / can* be able to fill their own bottles or drink from water fountains, but they [5]*won't / don't* be able to buy water in a plastic bottle. The museum thinks that if it [6]*stops / will stop* selling plastic water bottles, it [7]*helps / might help* reduce the amount of plastic in the ocean.

4 Circle the correct words.

If you [1]___ to protect the planet, what [2]___ you do? Lewis Pugh, the "human polar bear," swims long distances in some of the world's coldest waters to make people think about climate change. Sometimes the water is 0 °C, and he can stay in the water for only 20 minutes. If he [3]___ any longer, his body [4]___ working and he [5]___ probably die. Pugh wants governments to protect our oceans. He says that unless we [6]___ them now, we [7]___ them forever.

	a	b	c
1	want	wanted	would want
2	will	won't	would
3	stay	stayed	would stay
4	stops	stopped	would stop
5	doesn't	will	would
6	protect	will protect	would protect
7	lose	will lose	would lose

5 Complete the questions for the answers. Then write the questions and answers in the second conditional in your notebook. How does this change the meaning?

1 What will happen if *we don't reduce pollution*?
If we don't reduce pollution, we will destroy our beautiful oceans.

2 What will happen if ____________________
____________________? If we don't protect endangered species, they will disappear.

3 Can we protect the environment if
____________________?
If we make new laws, we can protect the environment.

Self-Assessment

I can talk about the planet Earth in English.
I can talk about natural environments.
I can use the first conditional.
I can use the second conditional.

LEARN TO ... UNDERSTAND HOW YOU LEARN

When you know what kind of language learner you are, you can decide how to improve your English.

1 Ask your partner the quiz questions and circle their answers.

Are You a Communicator or a Perfectionist?

Take our quiz to find out!

1 **In class, do you prefer to ...**
a speak in English with a partner?
b read and listen to a text on your own?

2 **If an English-speaking student visited your school, would you ...**
a chat with them to practice your English?
b only say hello to them or ask them simple questions like "How are you?"

3 **How do you feel when you're studying grammar in class?**
a I can't wait to do a different activity.
b I enjoy understanding and practicing the rules. It's my favorite thing!

4 **Your teacher gives you back a piece of written work. What do you do?**
a I quickly look at my grade and then put it in my bag.
b I read all of the corrections and comments carefully. They can help me do better next time.

5 **How do you feel when you make a mistake with your pronunciation?**
a If the person can still understand me, I don't mind.
b Embarrassed. I hate making mistakes.

6 **When you write or speak in English, do you ...**
a try to use new grammar and vocabulary?
b only use grammar and vocabulary you already know?

7 **If you did a presentation in English, would you ...**
a try to speak naturally without memorizing everything?
b memorize the whole presentation first?

2 Ask your partner how many *a* and *b* answers you have. Then read what kind of learner you are.

Mostly *a* answers: You're a communicator. You like speaking and if the other person understands you, you don't worry about making mistakes. This is good because you try to express what you want to say.

Mostly *b* answers: You're a perfectionist. You like to understand the rules of English and you hate making mistakes. This is good because you aim to speak and write correctly.

3 Do you agree with the description of you in Exercise 2? Why / Why not?

4 Which advice is for a communicator? Which is for a perfectionist?

1 You should try to use new language and practice speaking in class as much as possible. If you do, you'll be able to communicate more naturally. ____

2 You should pay more attention to grammar rules and to your teacher's corrections. If you do, you'll be able to speak and write more correctly. ____

5 What are the advantages and disadvantages of being a perfectionist, and of being a communicator?

SHAPE IT!

6 Look at the advice in Exercise 4. Tell your partner one thing you can do to improve your English.

6 How can inventions change our lives?

LEARNING OUTCOMES

I can ...

- understand texts about inventions
- give and follow instructions
- write a review of an invention
- understand how to use the passive
- talk about making things, materials, and containers
- use visualization techniques to remember vocabulary
- use background knowledge to understand texts and improve my speaking with games
- present an idea for an invention

Start It!

1 Look at the machine in the photo. What do you think it does?
2 Before you watch, what inventions are important to you?
3 What did Thomas Edison say when things went wrong? Watch and check.
4 What would you like to invent?

Watch video 6.1

p73

Grammar in Action 6.2

p75

Grammar in Action 6.3

p76

Everyday English 6.4

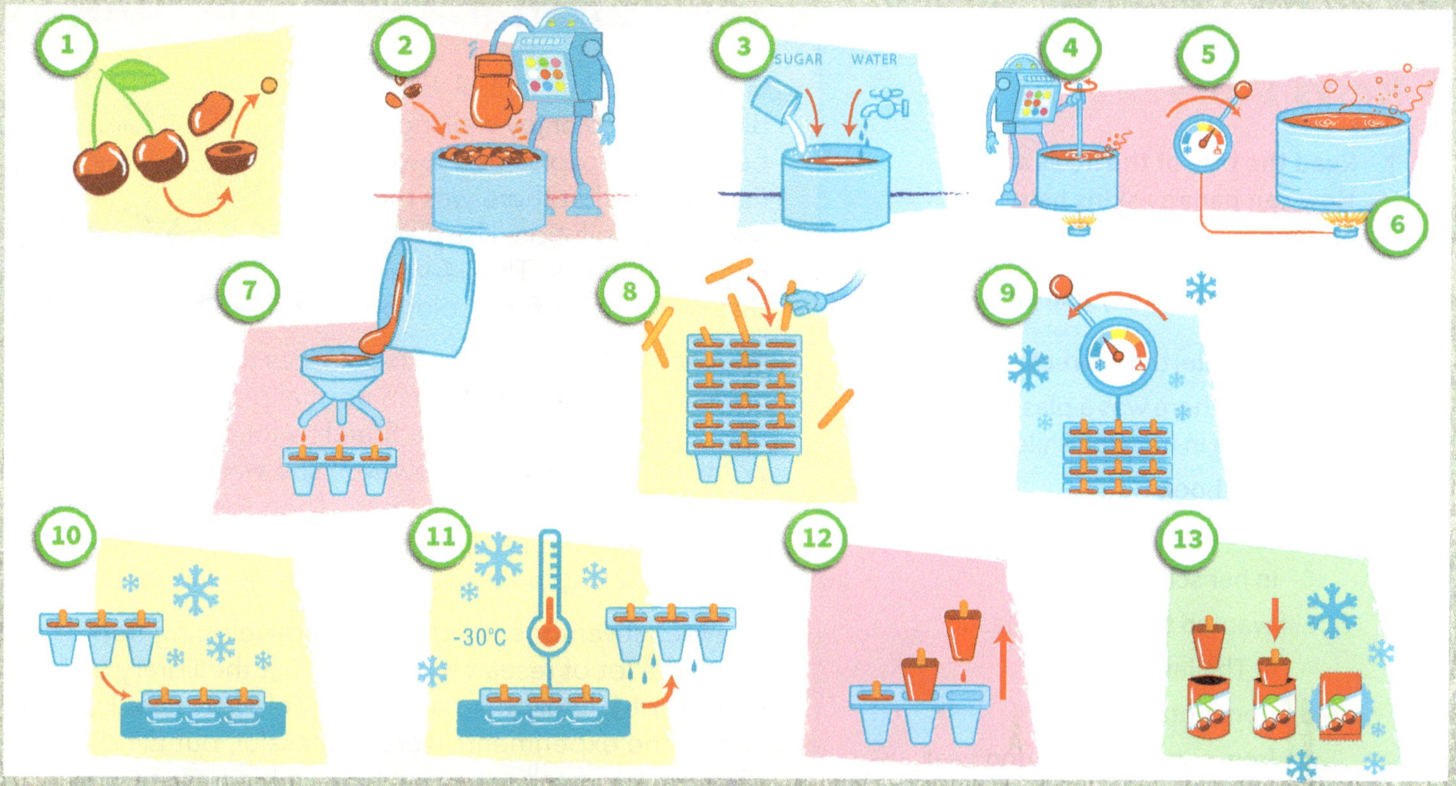

VOCABULARY

Making Things

6.01 **1 Listen to how you make an ice pop. Match the verbs with the pictures.**

add	☐	freeze	☐	pull	☐
boil	☐	increase	☐	reduce	☐
cover	☐	place	☐	remove	1
dip	☐	pour	☐	stir	☐
		press	☐		

6.02 **2 Listen again, check your answers to Exercise 1, and repeat.**

Pronunciation p142

LEARN TO LEARN

Visualizing

Thinking of an image to go with new words can help you remember their meaning.

3 Think of a strange or funny image for each of the verbs in Exercise 1. Tell your partner your ideas.

Use It!

4 Choose one of the things in the box and write how to make it in your notebook.

a candle   a cup of coffee   ice cream
perfume   a smoothie   soup

5 Tell your partner what to do. Can they guess what you are making?

First, you boil the water. Then you pour some milk into a cup and add some sugar …

Are you making a cup of coffee?

Explore It!

Guess the correct answer.

An … invented the ice pop in 1905.

a 11-year-old American boy

b 80-year-old Mexican man

c 18-year-old Spanish girl

Find another interesting fact about ice pops. Then write a question for your partner to answer.

READING

A News Story

1 **Read the title of the news story. How can banana skins help the environment?**

6.06 2 **Read the news story and check.**

3 EXAM **Circle the correct answers.**

1 Elif saw there was a plastic pollution problem in her city while she was …
   A at school.
   B walking by the Bosphorus.
   C in her science class.

2 Elif wanted to make bioplastic …
   A in Thailand.
   B from potatoes.
   C from something we don't eat.

3 Elif chose banana skins because …
   A they contain starch.
   B they're yellow.
   C she couldn't find enough potatoes.

4 Elif made bioplastic …
   A in her first experiment.
   B when she was 14.
   C from banana skins and some liquids.

4 **Match the words in bold with the meanings.**

1 did ____________
2 put in the trash can ____________
3 stop trying ____________
4 getting older ____________
5 search for ____________

Voice It!

5 **Discuss the questions.**

1 What do you think of Elif's invention?
2 Can you think of anything else we throw away that could be used again?

Finished? p123 Ex. 1

Teen's Banana Skin Invention

Growing up in Istanbul, Elif Bilgin used to enjoy walking beside the Bosphorus. However, Elif noticed that there was more and more pollution, like plastic bags, in the river. The 14-year-old decided to **look for** a solution.

At school, Elif learned that bioplastics are more environmentally friendly than normal plastics because they are made from starch. Starch is found in foods like potatoes and bananas. However, she wanted to use an organic material that isn't eaten. Then she learned that in Thailand, over 200 tons of banana skins are **thrown away** every day, and that's when she got her idea!

The teen inventor spent two years developing her idea. She did a lot of research online and at the library and **carried out** 12 experiments at school and in her kitchen. Not all the experiments were successful, but Elif didn't **give up**, and finally, she produced a bioplastic from banana skins. At 16, she won the Science in Action Award and the Inspired Idea Award at the Google Science Fair. Her invention could help make rivers, lakes, and oceans clean again. Since then, Elif has traveled the world telling people about her invention and has studied science in college so she can continue to make a difference in our world.

How is Elif's bioplastic made?

1 The banana skin is dipped in a special liquid.
2 The banana skin is placed in a glass and is heated for 30 minutes.
3 The banana skin is dried and is pressed into a paste.
4 Different liquids are added to the paste and the mixture is stirred.
5 The mixture is cooked in an oven and it is made into plastic.

Watch video 6.2
What does she use nail polish for?
How does she clean her keyboard?

GRAMMAR IN ACTION
Simple Present Passive

	Singular	Plural
+	The mixture [1]_______ **cooked** in an oven.	Different liquids **are added** to the paste.
-	She wanted to use an organic material that [2]_______ **eaten**.	Plastic bags **aren't recycled**.
?	How **is** Elif's bioplastic [3]_______?	How many banana skins **are thrown** away in Thailand every day?

1 Complete the examples the chart above. Use the news story on page 72 to help you.

2 Put the words in the correct order to make sentences.

1 found / starch / Where / is / ?
Where is starch found?

2 aren't / Most students / taught / to make bioplastic at school ____________

3 every day / experiments / How many / carried out / are / ? ____________

4 always / full of plastic bottles / The river / is ____________

3 Complete the text with the correct form of the verbs in parentheses. Then listen and check. 6.07

So, how [1] *is* a cell phone *made* (make)? Well, first the case [2]__________ (create) and then the circuit board [3]__________ (make). This is the most important part of the cell phone, as it runs the whole system. If the circuit board [4]__________ (not design) correctly, the phone won't work. Once the circuit board [5]__________ (finish), it [6]__________ (place) inside the case, and other parts, such as the screen, keypad, microphone, and speakers, [7]__________ (add). Finally, the phone [8]__________ (test) to check that it works before it [9]__________ (sell).

Use It!

4 Write questions in the simple present passive. Then answer them with a partner.

1 What ingredients / use / to make pasta?
What ingredients are used to make pasta?

2 Where / Arabic / speak? ____________

3 In which countries / insects / eat? ____________

4 What / make / from paper? ____________

5 Which places / visit / by tourists in your country? ____________

5 Work in pairs. Write two more questions in the simple present passive. Ask another pair.

____

____

Finished? p123 Ex. 2

VOCABULARY AND LISTENING

Materials and Containers

6.08 **1** **Use a word from each box to describe the photos (1–6). Then listen, check, and repeat.**

Materials
cardboard glass leather rubber ~~silk~~ tin
Containers
~~bag~~ box can case jar tube

1 

a silk bag

4 

2 

5 

3 

6 

Use It!

2 **Work in small groups. Use the words from Exercise 1 to write things you can see in your classroom.**

A Quiz Show

LEARN TO LEARN

Using Background Knowledge

Before you listen, think about what you already know about a topic. This helps you understand what you will hear.

3 **Tell your partner everything you know about two of the things in the photos.**

bagpipes

boomerang

piñata

chewing gum

6.09 **4** **Guess and circle the answers. Then listen and check.**

1. Where do bagpipes originally come from?
   a the U.S.A. b Europe c the Middle East
2. Where is the oldest boomerang from?
   a Australia b Poland c Brazil
3. Where do piñatas originally come from?
   a Argentina b Mexico c China
4. Which one of these inventions was an accident?
   a the ballpoint pen b the can opener c chewing gum

6.09 **5** **Listen again and complete the sentences.**

1. Anton thinks the first bagpipes came from ________.
2. The oldest boomerang is around ________ years old.
3. Marco Polo introduced ________ to Italy.
4. Thomas Adams wanted to make ________ from chicle.

Voice It!

6 **Discuss the questions.**

1. What information is the most surprising?
2. Which invention is the most useful? Why?

GRAMMAR IN ACTION

Simple Past Passive

Watch video 6.3
Who created chocolate chip cookies?
What was Ruth given?

	Singular	Plural
+	A boomerang **was discovered** in Poland.	Ice cream and pasta **were brought** to Italy from China [2]_______ Marco Polo.
–	The musical instrument [1]_______ **invented** in Europe.	Bagpipes **weren't found** in Europe first.
?	Where **was** the oldest boomerang **found**?	What objects [3]_______ **invented** by accident?

1 **Read the information below. Then complete the examples in the chart above.**

Get It Right!

We use **by** to show who or what is doing the action in passive sentences.

The students are taught by Ms. Goodall.

We do not use **by** when it's not important to know who or what is doing the action.

The newspaper is delivered every morning ~~by the newspaper carrier~~.

6.10 **2** **Circle the correct form of the verb. Then listen and check.**

Easter Island, or Rapa Nui, [1]*(is)* / *was* located in the Pacific Ocean, about 3,500 km from Chile. The small island [2]*first inhabited* / *was first inhabited* around 1,000 years ago. In 1722, the island [3]*discovered* / *was discovered* by a Dutch explorer. He [4]*found* / *was found* a small population of about 3,000 people and nearly 900 mysterious statues around the island. The giant head statues, or Moai, [5]*built* / *were built* from volcanic stone and [6]*placed* / *were placed* along the coast with their backs to the ocean. But how [7]*were* / *did* these enormous statues moved around the island 1,000 years ago?

3 **Rewrite the sentences in the simple past passive.**

1 Isaac Newton invented the cat door.
The cat door was invented by Isaac Newton.

2 A dentist invented cotton candy.
Cotton candy _______________________________.

3 Ernö Rubik didn't design the Rubik's Cube to be a toy.
The Rubik's Cube _______________________________.

4 People in Norway didn't eat bananas until 1905.
Bananas _______________________________.

Use It!

4 **Work in pairs. Write questions in the simple past passive about your country 50 years ago.**

1 music / listen to / by teenagers?
What music was listened to by teenagers in your country 50 years ago?

2 sports / play / at school? _______________________________

3 shows / watch / on TV? _______________________________

4 special days / celebrate / at home? _______________________________

5 subjects / study / at school? _______________________________

Finished? p123 Ex. 3

SPEAKING

Giving and Following Instructions

6.11 **1 Listen to the conversation. What does Alicia make?**

ALICIA	Hey Juan, I saw a video the other day of a great invention that was made from a balloon. Do you want me to show you how to make it?
JUAN	Yeah, go for it!
ALICIA	Well, [1] <u>first of all</u>, take a balloon, any old balloon, any color you want.
JUAN	OK. [2] ____________?
ALICIA	Then blow up the balloon and hold it tightly so that the air doesn't escape.
JUAN	OK, that's easy.
ALICIA	[3] ____________ the balloon's inflated, place it on a table in front of you and place your phone on the balloon with the screen facing upward.
JUAN	OK, I get it. [4] ____________?
ALICIA	[5] ____________ kind of tricky. Press the phone down on the balloon. Don't let go of the balloon and don't let the air out too quickly. In the video, the air came out really slowly.
JUAN	Hang on a sec! [6] ____________. So, push down carefully until all the air is removed.
ALICIA	Exactly. [7] ____________! A cell phone case!
JUAN	[8] ____________. Hey, that's so cool!

6.11 **2 Complete the conversation with the phrases from the *Useful Language* box. Then listen again and check.**

Useful Language

Giving Instructions	Following Instructions
And there you have it!	Let me get this straight.
~~First of all, …~~	Oh, I see.
Once (something is done), …	Then what?
The next part's …	What's next?

3 Match the words and phrases (1–5) with the phrases in the *Everyday English* box.

1 Wait a minute!
2 difficult
3 I understand.
4 Do it!
5 any (informal)

Watch video 6.4
Everyday English

any old …	☐	Go for it!	☐
Hang on a sec!	☐	I get it.	☐
kind of tricky	☐		

PLAN

4 Read the conversation again. Complete Alicia's notes about how to make something from a balloon.

What you need: ____________

What you do first: ____________

What you do next: ____________

What you do last: ____________

What happens in the end: ____________

5 Work in pairs. Plan a conversation about how to do something. Use the ideas below or your own.

cook some food make a paper plane play a sport

SPEAK

6 Practice a conversation. Remember to use the simple present passive and phrases from the *Useful Language* and *Everyday English* boxes.

CHECK

7 Work with another pair. Listen to their conversation and decide what they are talking about.

BRINGING COLOR TO A GRAY WORLD

HOME | STORIES | PHOTOS

Millions of people around the world are color blind. They can't see some colors, such as red, green, or blue. Some people who are color blind can't see any colors at all, so the world looks very different. But now there are special glasses to help color-blind people. The glasses look like normal glasses, but the lenses are made from special glass or plastic. The glasses separate colors, such as red and green, so that people can see them. When they are worn by color-blind people, they can see colors they have never seen before.

What I like about them is that they look really cool. There are sunglasses, glasses for children, and sports sunglasses. However, I should point out that the glasses are really expensive. Overall, I think they are an amazing invention that can help millions of people see our beautiful world.

WRITING

A Review

1 **Look at the photo. What do the glasses do? Read the review and check.**

2 **Put a–f in the order they appear in the review.**

a ☐ a description of the invention
b ☐ how the invention works
c ☐ a disadvantage
d ☐ the reviewer's general opinion
e ☐ what the reviewer likes
f [1] who the invention is for

3 **Cover the review and complete the sentences in the *Useful Language* box. Then read it again and check.**

Useful Language

The glasses look like [1] ____________, but the lenses are made from [2] ____________.
What I like about them is [3] ____________ ____________.
However, I should point out that [4] ____________ ____________.
Overall, I think they are [5] ____________ ____________.

PLAN

4 **Write your own review of an amazing invention. Think of the invention. Write notes.**

Who the invention is for: ____________
How it works: ____________
The advantages: ____________
One disadvantage: ____________
Your opinion: ____________

5 **Decide what information to include. Use the information in Exercise 2 to help you.**

WRITE

6 **Write your review. Remember to include the parts of the review from Exercise 2, the passive, and phrases from the *Useful Language* box.**

CHECK

7 **Do you ...**

- describe the invention and who it's for?
- say what the advantages and disadvantages are?
- give your general opinion?

Finished? p123 Ex. 4

TECHNOLOGY PROJECT

A Presentation

6.12 **1 Match the headings (a–d) with the slides (1–4). Then listen to the presentation and check.**

a A Problem and Some Solutions
b How Our Invention Works
c Problems at Our School
d Our Design

2 Discuss the questions.

1 What is the invention called? Why?
2 What problem does it solve?
3 What is the invention made from?
4 How does it work?
5 Is it a good idea? Why / Why not?

How to Brainstorm

3 Put the stages in order.

a Compare ideas in a group. ☐
b Have a time limit. ☐
c Make a list of as many ideas as possible. ☐
d Put two ideas together if necessary. ☐
e Think of ideas on your own. ☐
f Use your imagination and creativity to think of ideas. ☐
g Write down or draw your ideas. ☐

6.13 **4 Listen again to the students presenting the first two slides and check your answers. Which stage is not mentioned?** ____________

- too much homework
- too many exams
- not enough PE
- too many unhealthy snacks
- not enough recycling of plastic bottles
- too many books to carry

1 ☐

2 ☐

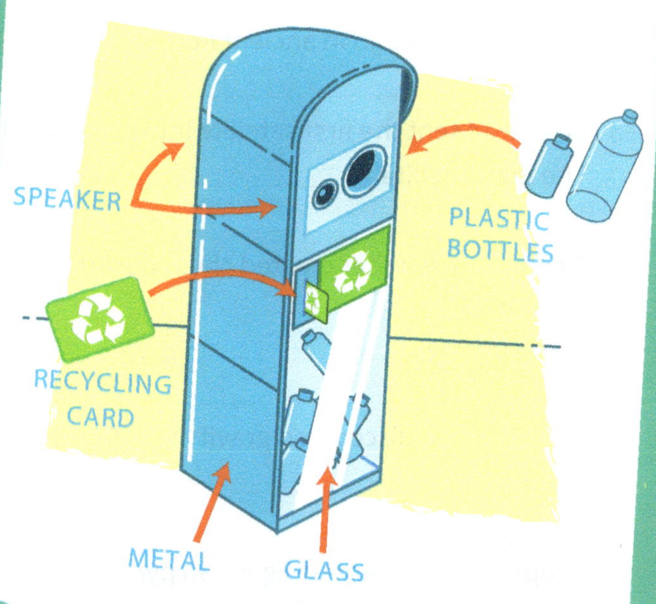

3 ☐

PLAN

5 Work in groups. Complete the steps. Use the stages from Exercise 3.

- Make a list of problems people have at school or at home.
- Choose one problem and think of a lot of solutions.
- Choose one solution and create an invention. Use Exercise 2 to help you.
- Draw the design. What materials are used? How does it work?
- Make four slides to present your invention.
- Decide who presents each slide.
- Listen to everyone in the group practice their slide and help them improve.

PRESENT

6 Present your slides to the class. Remember to say how the invention solves a problem and how it works.

CHECK

7 Listen to your classmates' presentations. Do they include all the information from Exercise 2?

4 ☐

6 REVIEW

VOCABULARY

1 Match the verbs with the definitions.

dip increase place reduce remove stir

1 put something in a position ______
2 put something in a liquid ______
3 make a temperature higher ______
4 make something less ______
5 take something away ______
6 move a liquid with a spoon ______

2 Write the letters in the correct order to make words for materials and containers.

1 gba ______
2 drbdrcraoa ______
3 nit ______
4 slsag ______
5 xob ______
6 thealre ______
7 brbreu ______
8 lkis ______
9 nac ______
10 scae ______
11 raj ______
12 bute ______

GRAMMAR IN ACTION

3 Complete the text with the simple present passive form of the verbs in parentheses.

Street festivals and celebrations are fun, but they also create a lot of trash, which [1]______ (not put) in trash cans, but [2]______ just ______ (throw) on the floor. One inventor in Portugal has solved this problem with his Garbage Jukebox – a trash can that plays music. The machine [3]______ (not power) by electricity, but by trash, so when a drink can or bottle [4]______ (place) in the machine, music [5]______ (play) – 30 seconds for each can and one minute for each bottle. What a great idea!

4 Rewrite the sentences in the simple past passive.

1 Someone discovered unique fingerprints in 1823.
Unique fingerprints ______
______.

2 People spoke Latin in ancient Rome.
Latin ______.

3 Scientists sent the first satellite into space in 1957.
The first satellite ______
______.

4 A comic book writer created chess boxing in one of his stories.
Chess boxing ______
______.

5 Isaac Newton discovered gravity in 1664.
Gravity ______
______.

6 People built the largest Egyptian pyramid in Giza, near Cairo.
The largest Egyptian pyramid ______
______.

Self-Assessment

I can talk about making things in English.
I can talk about materials and containers.
I can use the simple present passive.
I can use the simple past passive.

LEARN TO ... IMPROVE YOUR SPEAKING WITH GAMES

When you play speaking games, you can relax and use English in different situations.

1 Which of the situations below is the most difficult for you? Why?

a describing something in English when you don't know the word

b asking questions in the past, present, active, and passive

c speaking in English without thinking in your language first

2 Play *Forbidden Words* in pairs. Take turns describing each word in bold without using the other words on the card.

box
put
cardboard
keep
open

soccer
sport
play
ball
team

phone
call
screen
number
app

school
study
student
teacher
learn

This is an object. It's usually square. It's often made of, err, a kind of stiff paper.

Is it a box?

Yes! Your turn.

3 Work with a partner and make eight *Forbidden Words* cards like the ones in Exercise 2. Swap your cards with another pair. Then read the rules and play the game.

1 Put the cards face down.

2 Take four cards each. Don't show your partner.

3 Describe the word on the card without using the forbidden words.

4 Your partner gets one point if they guess the word in less than one minute.

5 The player with the most points at the end of the game wins.

4 Stefan and Anne are playing *Guess Who?* Stefan is thinking of someone. Anne has two minutes to guess the person. She can only ask *Yes/No* questions. Write the person.

ANNE Is this person a man?
STEFAN No, it isn't.
ANNE Is it a woman?
STEFAN Hmm … not a woman, no.
ANNE Is it a girl then?
STEFAN Yes.
ANNE Have I met her?
STEFAN I don't think so!
ANNE Have we studied her in this book?
STEFAN Yes, we have.
ANNE Did she invent something to help clean rivers?
STEFAN Yes, she did.
ANNE Was her invention made from banana skins?
STEFAN Yes, it was.
ANNE I know! Is it ______________________ ______________________?

5 Play *Guess Who?* with a partner. Take turns thinking of a person.

SHAPE IT!

6 Discuss with a partner. Look again at Exercise 1 and answer the questions.

1 Which things a–c have you practiced in *Forbidden Words*? __________

2 Which things a–c have you practiced in *Guess Who?* __________

7 What do you celebrate?

LEARNING OUTCOMES

I can ...

- understand texts about a folktale and festivals
- invite someone to a party
- write an email to a friend
- understand how to use the past perfect and reported speech
- talk about festivals and live music
- mark word stress, predict information, identify and understand prefixes and suffixes , and challenge yourself to do more in class

Start It!

1 Look at the photo. Would you like to go to this festival?
2 Before you watch, what kind of things do people celebrate at festivals?
3 When was the first Snowbombing Festival? Watch and check.
4 What is your favorite festival? Describe it.

Watch video 7.1

p85

Grammar in Action 7.2

p87

Grammar in Action 7.3

p88

Everyday English 7.4

p90

Globetrotters 7.5

VOCABULARY

Festivals

7.01 **1 Match the words with the photos (1–9) and definitions (10–12). Then listen, check, and repeat.**

atmosphere	☐	fireworks	☐
ceremony	☐	float	☐
costume	1	lantern	☐
crowd	☐	parade	☐
decoration	☐	program	☐
fair	☐	stall	☐

10 the feeling in a place or situation
11 an event that happens on important occasions
12 a large group of people in one place

LEARN TO LEARN

Stress Patterns

Knowing the stress pattern of a word can help you pronounce it and hear it when people say it.

7.02 **2 Complete the chart with words from Exercise 1 according to their stress pattern. Then listen, check, and repeat.**

1	oO	parade
2	Oo	________, ________, ________, ________
3	Ooo	________
4	Oooo	________
5	ooOo	________

Pronunciation p142

7.05 **3 Listen to the conversation and (circle) the words in Exercise 1 that you hear. Then work in pairs to describe the festival.**

The Caribbean Parade and Festival is a celebration of Caribbean culture in Montreal, Canada ...

Use It!

4 Write sentences in your notebook about a festival using words from Exercise 1. Then read your sentences to a partner.

In my town, there's a parade every year. Everyone wears costumes and there are decorations in the streets.

Explore It!

Guess the correct answer.

The biggest parade and festival in the world is held in ...

a Venice. b Rio de Janeiro. c New Orleans.

Find another interesting fact about a festival. Then write a question for your partner to answer.

READING
A Folktale

A Princess, a Farmer, and a Bridge of Birds

Throughout history, different cultures have looked up at the stars in the night sky and told stories about them. The ancient Greeks told stories about heroes, and the Native Americans about bears and fishermen. In Japan, people still tell the story of Altair and Vega, two very special stars.

Once upon a time, there was a princess named Orihime. She made beautiful clothes for her father, the Sky King, while she sat on the **bank** of the *Amanogawa River* (the Milky Way). Orihime had always loved her work, but she wanted to find a husband, so her father introduced her to a farmer named Hikoboshi. Hikoboshi took care of cows on the other side of the river. The princess and the farmer fell in love and got married. However, they hadn't been together long when Orihime stopped making clothes and Hikoboshi forgot about his cows.

The Sky King was **furious**. "You will never meet again," he told them, and he sent them to opposite sides of the river. But when he saw how **heartbroken** his daughter had become, he changed his mind. "If you do your jobs well," he said, "you can meet once a year, on the seventh day of the seventh month." However, the first time the couple tried to meet, they couldn't cross the river. "I want to see him!" cried Orihime. Almost immediately, a **flock** of magpies came and made a bridge with their wings. Now people say if it rains on July 7, the magpies can't come and Orihime and Hikoboshi have to wait another year.

Every year, this story is celebrated in Japan as the *Tanabata* – the Star Festival. There are parades, fireworks, lanterns, and stalls with traditional food, and people write their wishes on *tanzaku* (pieces of colorful paper), remembering how Orihime's wish had come true.

1 Look at the title and the pictures. What do you think happens in the story?

7.06 **2** Read the folktale and check.

3 Are the sentences *T* (true) or *F* (false)?

1. All cultures have told the same stories about the stars. F
2. The Sky King wanted Orihime to get married. ___
3. After Orihime and Hikoboshi married, Orihime continued making clothes for her father. ___
4. Orihime and Hikoboshi try to meet every year. ___
5. During *Tanabata*, Japanese people say what they hope will happen in the future. ___

4 Match the words in **bold** with the definitions.

1. the land at the side of a river ___________
2. a group of birds ___________
3. very angry ___________
4. very, very sad ___________

Voice It!

5 Discuss the questions.

1. Do you think the king was fair to his daughter?
2. Why are folktales important?
3. Are there similar festivals in your country?

Finished? p124 Ex. 1

Watch video 7.2
What's another name for Yuri's night?
Why was the DJ still able to play music?

GRAMMAR IN ACTION
Past Perfect

+	When he saw how heartbroken his daughter [1] ________ **become**,	he **changed** his mind.
–	They **hadn't** [2] ________ together long	when Orihime **stopped** making clothes.
?	**Had** the parade already **started**	when you **arrived**?

1 **Complete the examples in the chart above. Use the folktale on page 84 to help you.**

2 **Match the sentence beginnings with the endings.**

1 I'd studied German before I went to Germany, [c]
2 I was very hungry when I got home from soccer, [ ]
3 She was cold [ ]
4 He didn't come to see the new movie [ ]

a because she hadn't brought her jacket.
b because he'd already seen it.
c but I learned more while I was there.
d so I was pleased that my dad had cooked dinner.

3 **Complete the sentences with the correct form of the past perfect.**

1 When we got to the park, (the fireworks / finish).
When we got to the park, the fireworks had finished.

2 (Jaime / never / go) to a music festival, so he was really excited.
____
____

3 (you / hear) about the Caribbean Parade before you came to Montreal?
____
____

4 After (she / buy) some food at a stall, she went to watch the parade.
____
____

5 It was nine o'clock, but (the event / not / start) yet.
____
____

7.07 **4** **Complete the text with the correct form of the verbs in parentheses. Then listen and check.**

Today was almost a disaster. My friends and I were going to the Albuquerque International Balloon Fiesta, but when we [1] got (get) there, I [2] ________ (realize) I [3] ________ (not bring) my ticket. I [4] ________ (leave) it at home. At first, I [5] ________ (not know) what to do, but then I [6] ________ (call) my mom. Luckily, she [7] ________ (not leave) the house to go to work yet, so she [8] ________ (find) the ticket, [9] ________ (take) a photo of it, and [10] ________ (send) me the photo. Anyway, it [11] ________ (be) an amazing event. I [12] ________ (never see) so many balloons before. The sky was full of them!

Use It!

5 **Write questions about what you knew before you started this book. Ask and answer.**

1 … (hear) of the *Tanabata* festival?
Before you started this book, had you heard of the *Tanabata* festival?

2 … (study) the past perfect?
____

3 … (read) about color-blind glasses?
____

4 … (think) about how astronauts exercise?
____

Finished? p124 Ex. 2

VOCABULARY AND LISTENING

Music Festivals and Live Music

7.08 **1 Match the words with the definitions. Then listen, check, and repeat.**

band members	☐	headliner	☐	tent	1
campsite	☐	stage	☐	track	☐
encore	☐	supporting act	☐	venue	☐
gig	☐				

1 something you sleep in outdoors
2 where a special event happens
3 the main band at a festival
4 a song or piece of music
5 the musicians in a group
6 an extra song at the end of a show
7 where musicians perform
8 where people can stay in tents
9 a music performance
10 not the main artist

2 EXAM **Write the correct answer in the gap. Write one or two words from Exercise 1.**

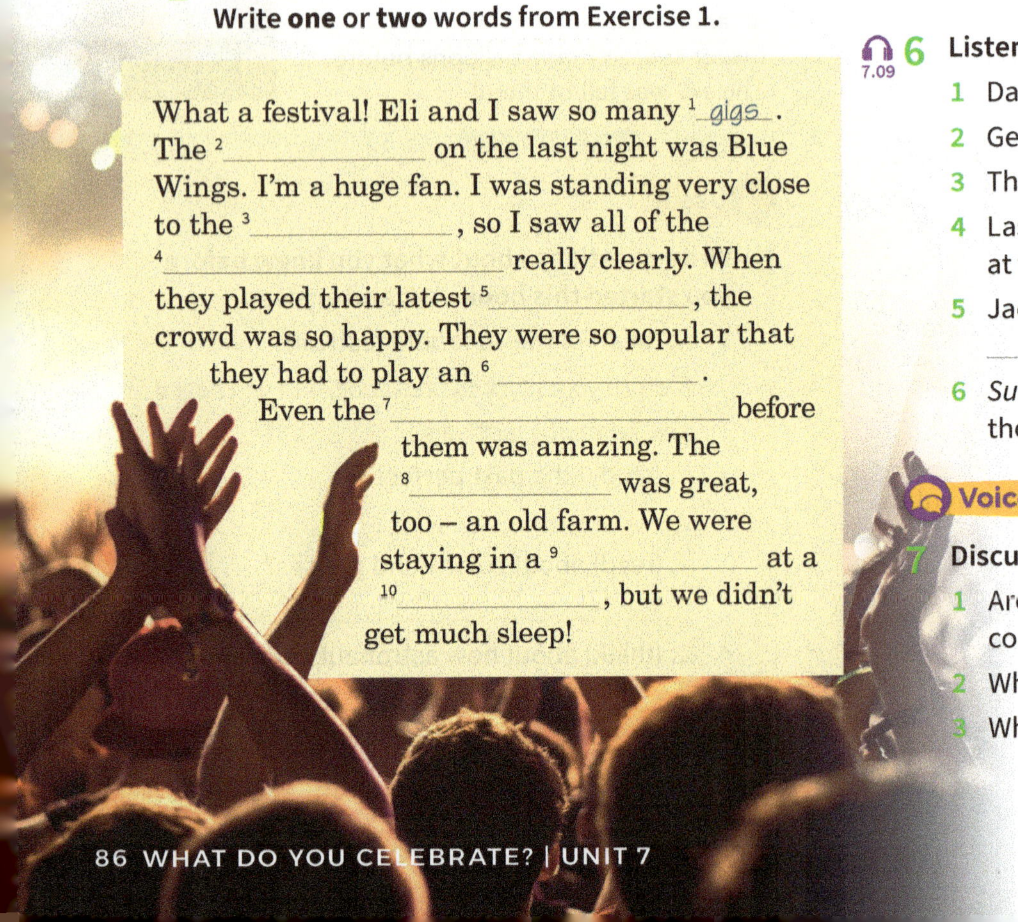

What a festival! Eli and I saw so many [1] gigs. The [2] ______ on the last night was Blue Wings. I'm a huge fan. I was standing very close to the [3] ______, so I saw all of the [4] ______ really clearly. When they played their latest [5] ______, the crowd was so happy. They were so popular that they had to play an [6] ______. Even the [7] ______ before them was amazing. The [8] ______ was great, too – an old farm. We were staying in a [9] ______ at a [10] ______, but we didn't get much sleep!

Use It!

3 Imagine you went to a music festival recently. Write notes about it using the vocabulary from Exercise 1. Tell your partner.

______
______
______
______

A Conversation

7.09 **4 Listen to the conversation. What are Daryl and Jackie going to do in the summer?**

LEARN TO LEARN

Predicting Information

Skim the questions before you listen and try to predict what kind of information you need.

5 Look at Exercise 6. What kind of information is missing from each of the sentences?

a an object   b a place   c a number

1 c   3 ___   5 ___
2 ___   4 ___   6 ___

7.09 **6 Listen again and complete the sentences.**

1 Daryl's cousin went to Morocco two years ago.
2 Gemma sold ______ at a stall.
3 There are ______ main stages at *SumFun*.
4 Last year more than ______ people were at the festival.
5 Jackie can only remember the name of ______ band.
6 *SumFun* has always taken place at a venue in the ______.

Voice It!

7 Discuss the questions.

1 Are there any famous music festivals in your country? Where are they?
2 What other jobs do volunteers do at a festival?
3 Which jobs would you most like to do? Why?

Watch video 7.3
Where was the rock festival that her neighbor went to? What advice did the neighbor give her?

GRAMMAR IN ACTION
Reported Statements

	Direct Speech	Reported Speech
Simple Present	"The people [1] are really friendly."	He said the people **were** really friendly.
Present Continuous	"I[2] ________ about volunteering."	She said she **was thinking** about volunteering.
Simple Past	"I [3] ________ Blue Wings."	She said she **had seen** Blue Wings.
Present Perfect	"I[4] ________ really hard."	She told me she **had worked** really hard.

1 **Complete the examples in the chart above.**

2 **Circle the correct answers. Then listen and check.** 7.10

Mark told me he [1]*was going* (circled) / *had gone* to Thailand next week. He said he [2]*has been* / *was* really excited and that it [3]*will be* / *was* the only thing he [4]*can* / *could* think about. He told me he [5]*had bought* / *bought* his ticket last week and he [6]*'d downloaded* / *'s downloaded* an app to learn Thai yesterday. He said he [7]*packed* / *'d packed* his suitcase this morning and that he [8]*was* / *'d be* in Bangkok next Monday. He said he [9]*went* / *was going* to meet his sister there. He told me he [10]*had written* / *'d write* and tell us all about it.

Get It Right!

We use words like *me*, *he*, *her* after **tell**, but not after **say**.

He told me he couldn't.

He said he couldn't.

NOT ~~He said me he couldn't.~~

3 **Rewrite the sentences as reported speech.**

1 "I went to an incredible festival." She told me she'd been to an incredible festival.
2 "I don't have a costume." He said ________.
3 "I'm waiting for the parade to start." She told me ________.
4 "I can't see the stage because there are too many people." He said ________.
5 "Don't forget to send me some photos." He said ________.

4 **Rewrite the reported speech as direct speech. Then check in the story on page 84.**

1 He told them they would never meet again.
____
2 He said that if they did their jobs well, they could meet once a year.
____
3 She said she wanted to see him.
____

Use It!

5 **Work in pairs. Ask and answer the questions.**

1 What sports do you like?
2 What did you do last weekend?
3 What have you eaten today?

6 **Work in different pairs. Report what your partner said in Exercise 5.**

Finished? p124 Ex. 3

SPEAKING
Inviting a Friend to a Party

7.11 **1 Listen to the conversation. What does Ryan think he's doing on Saturday?**

JOSH Hey, Lara! [1]What are you up to on Saturday?
LARA Why? Is something happening?
JOSH It's Ryan's 17th. We're organizing a little celebration for him. Why don't you join us?
LARA Sure, [2]____________. I'd forgotten it was his birthday. Where is it?
JOSH It's at my place, but don't say anything to him. It's a surprise.
LARA A surprise party? Really?
JOSH Yeah, he told me once he'd never had one before, so I thought, why not? He thinks we're going to a gig.
LARA OK. I won't say a word. [3]________________________?
JOSH It kicks off at six, but you can come when you like.
LARA OK, [4]____________ around seven. [5]________________________?
JOSH Why don't you bring some snacks?
LARA OK. What about a present? Should I get him something?
JOSH He said he wanted a new backpack. We can buy him one together if you like.
LARA Sure. Count me in.
JOSH Great! See you there, then! And tell your brother to come. The more the merrier!

7.11 **2 Complete the conversation with the phrases from the *Useful Language* box. Then listen again and check.**

Useful Language

I'd love to.	I'll be there (at/around) …
Should I bring anything?	~~What are you up to … ?~~
What time should I be there?	

3 Complete the sentences with the phrases in the *Everyday English* box.

1 ________________________ I'm good at keeping secrets.
2 Of course I want to come with you. ________________________
3 Invite everyone you know – ________________________.
4 Why don't we meet ________________?
5 ________________ ten o'clock.

Watch video 7.4
Everyday English

at my place	Count me in.
It kicks off at …	I won't say a word.
The more the merrier.	

PLAN

4 Read the conversation in Exercise 1 again. Write notes about the party.

What type of party is it? ________________

Where and when is it? ________________

What should people bring? ________________

5 Work in pairs. Plan a conversation about a party. Use the ideas from Exercise 4.

SPEAK

6 Practice a conversation. Remember to use the past perfect, reported speech, and phrases from the *Useful Language* and *Everyday English* boxes.

CHECK

7 Work with another pair. Listen to their conversation and answer the questions from Exercise 4.

WRITING
An Email to a Friend

To Mason

Hi Mason,

Thanks for your email. It was great to hear from you!

Yesterday was my sister's graduation. I'd never been to a graduation before. It was a little different from what I'd expected! The ceremony took place at the University of Venice in Italy. Everyone was wearing formal clothes and there were some really long speeches. Then the students went up to the stage to collect their certificates. I was so proud of Sally when she got hers!

Later there was a party by one of the canals. All the students had put on crowns, an ancient symbol of victory. The craziest thing was that everyone was throwing eggs at each other. Sally said it was a tradition from Venice. I told her it felt more like a festival than a graduation!

Anyway, that's all from me. Write back soon!

Bye for now,

Gloria

1 **Look at the photo. What is the girl wearing? Read Gloria's email and check.**

2 **Put a–e in the order they appear in Gloria's email.**

- a ☐ goodbye
- b ☐ thanks for writing
- c ☐ greeting
- d ☐ description of the ceremony
- e ☐ request for a reply

3 **Look at the phrases in the *Useful Language* box. Are they opening or closing phrases? Write *O* (opening) or *C* (closing).**

Useful Language

- a Anyway, that's all from me. ___
- b Bye for now, ___
- c It was great to hear from you! ___
- d Thanks for your email. ___
- e Write back soon! ___

PLAN

4 **Write an email about a ceremony. Think of a ceremony you have been to. Write notes.**

What was it for? ______________________

____

Where was it? ______________________

____

What did people wear? ______________________

____

What did people do? ______________________

____

5 **Decide what information to include. Use the information in Exercise 2 to help you.**

WRITE

6 **Write your email. Remember to include the structure from Exercise 2, the past perfect, reported speech, and phrases from the *Useful Language* box.**

CHECK

7 **Do you …**

- have a greeting and a goodbye?
- describe the ceremony?
- request a reply?

Finished? p124 Ex. 4

AROUND THE WORLD

READING
A Travel Blog

1 Look at the photo of the lanterns. What do you know about Chinese festivals?

7.12 2 Read and match the photo with one of the festivals in the blog. ________

Globetrotters
Watch video 7.5
A Monkey Buffet

- Can you think of any festivals with animals?
- When does the Monkey Buffet Festival take place?
- Do you agree that this is a good reason to celebrate? Why / Why not?

Ollie in China

Chinese people love to celebrate, so they have a lot of festivals throughout the year. Here are my top three.

1
Harbin Ice and Snow Sculpture Festival

When I was a kid, I used to think my snowy creations were excellent, but they were nothing compared to what I saw at the Harbin International Ice and Snow Sculpture Festival. Artists from around the world come to the event and compete to build the most beautiful sculptures from snow and ice. Many were covered in colorful lights. In 2007, a group of Canadian artists made a sculpture of Niagara Falls that was 250 meters long and used 13,000 m^3 of snow. Nobody had ever made such a huge snow sculpture before!

2
Chinese New Year

Did you know that about 20 percent of the world's population celebrates Chinese New Year? But it doesn't take place on January 1, it starts just before spring. It's a time when families pay respects to their ancestors and exchange gifts. In China, red is a lucky color, so there are red decorations everywhere, red lanterns in the street, and poems in bright red paint on the doors of houses. People also enjoy traditional food. *Tangyuan*, the sweet rice balls I tried in Beijing, were one of the most delicious things I'd ever eaten.

3
Dragon Boat Festival

When my Chinese friends told me they wanted to take me to see a dragon boat race in Hong Kong, I thought, dragons in boats?! But no – I'd misunderstood! The boats are wooden and decorated as dragons. They're about 25–30 meters long and look awesome. Each boat has a team of up to 60 powerful rowers. People have celebrated the festival since 273 BCE! They say that good luck and happiness come to the winners. While we were watching, I ate *zongzi*, a traditional dish made of rice and bamboo leaves. It was really good!

3 **Write the name of the festival(s).**

1 People give presents. *Chinese New Year*

2 You can take part in a competition. ________

3 People celebrate with food. ________

4 It is over 1,700 years old. ________

4 **What do these numbers in the blog refer to?**

a 20 *The percentage of the world's population that celebrates Chinese New Year.*

b 250 ________

c 25–30 ________

d 60 ________

e 13,000 m^3 ________

Voice It!

5 Discuss the questions.

1 During Chinese New Year, families pay respects to their ancestors. Why is this important?
2 In what ways do people show respect to others?
3 Who do you most respect in your life?

LEARN TO LEARN

Suffixes

Suffixes can help expand your vocabulary.

6 Find the adjectives from nouns 1–5 in the blog and underline the suffixes. Then use the suffixes to make adjectives from nouns 6–10.

1 beauty *beautiful*
2 color ______
3 luck ______
4 power ______
5 snow ______
6 care ______
7 dirt ______
8 health ______
9 hope ______
10 thought ______

Explore It!

Guess the correct answer.

In the Chinese zodiac, every New Year is represented by an animal. Which of these animals is not in the zodiac?

a lion b monkey c snake

Find another interesting fact about China. Then write a question for your partner to answer.

SHAPE IT!

CULTURE PROJECT

A Travel Blog

A travel blog has short texts about one or more locations.
In groups, write a travel blog post about a festival.

Teacher's Resource Bank

7 REVIEW

VOCABULARY

1 **Complete the sentences with the words in the box.**

ceremony fireworks floats parade

Did you know ...

1 The world's biggest ______________ takes place in Manhattan in November. It is famous for its huge balloons.

2 The word for ______________ in Japanese means "fire-flower."

3 During the opening ______________ of the Olympic Games, Greek athletes always enter the stadium first.

4 During the Bloemencorso Parade in the Netherlands, ______________ decorated with eight million flowers drive through the streets.

2 **Match the parts of the poster with the words.**

band members ☐ gig ☐ headliner ☐
supporting acts ☐ venue ☐

GRAMMAR IN ACTION

3 **Answer the questions with the past perfect.**

1 Why was Cheng so happy? (his team / win / the match)

____

2 Why didn't Freddy buy a sandwich? (leave / his money / at home)

____

3 Why did they come home late? (miss / the bus)

____

4 Why was Lisa bored? (see / the movie / before)

____

4 **Rewrite the sentences as reported speech.**

1 "There's a festival in the park," Jacob told me.

____

2 "Don't touch my things!" Nellie told her brother.

____

3 "I've never been to a festival before," said Mike.

____

4 "You can watch the fireworks with my family," said Chloe.

____

5 "I'll visit Grandma on the weekend," said Claire.

____

Self-Assessment

I can talk about festivals in English.	☹	😐	☺
I can talk about music festivals and live music.	☹	😐	☺
I can use the past perfect.	☹	😐	☺
I can use reported statements.	☹	😐	☺

LEARN TO ... CHALLENGE YOURSELF TO DO MORE IN CLASS

You can feel more positive about learning by challenging yourself to do more. When you make an effort, you get better results.

1 Charlotte and Gael finish a project before their classmates. How can they use their time well? Why?

a do their homework for another subject
b do extra English activities together or alone
c chat in their language

2 Charlotte and Gael decide to play *Blank!* to practice vocabulary. Read how to play. Write the *Blank!* words.

How to Play *Blank!*

- Choose a text you've read in this book.
- **Player A:** Read the first half of the text to Player B but say "*blank*" instead of some words.
- **Player B:** Try to remember the missing words.
- Swap roles.

OK, Gael, the Japanese folktale. Throughout Blank!, different cultures ...

History!

That's right. ... different cultures have looked up at the Blank! [1] ______ in the night sky and told Blank! [2] ______ about them.

3 Nathan and Rita finish a speaking activity before their classmates. How can they use the extra minutes well? Why?

a ask each other some more questions in English
b clean up their desks
c listen to the other pairs

4 Student A: talk for one minute about a topic from the box. Student B: when your partner finishes, ask three questions about the topic. Then swap roles.

a folktale I know an interesting festival I have been to my favorite TV show

5 George finishes the last activity of the class before his classmates. He makes a mini-plan for the next class. Complete his plan with the words in the box.

grammar	practice	vocabulary

Mini-Plan
In the next class, I want to ...
use this [1] ______ : past perfect
use this [2] ______ : program, atmosphere, crowd
and [3] ______ : asking questions

SHAPE IT!

6 Choose a reading text from Units 1–7 and play *Blank!*

7 Make a mini-plan for the next class like the one in Exercise 5. Use and practice these things in the next class.

8 What is education?

LEARNING OUTCOMES

I can ...

- understand texts about dangerous journeys to school and school rules
- explain and ask about rules
- write an essay about rules at school
- talk about obligation, permission, and prohibition
- talk about school, behavior, and attitude
- personalize vocabulary, think about content before listening, and ask for help when you don't understand.
- design a school brochure

Start It!

1 Look at the photo. Where do you think the girl is going? Why?

2 Before you watch, how are schools different around the world?

3 In which country do students have the most homework? Watch and check.

4 Which other subjects would you like to study at school?

Watch video 8.1

p97

Grammar in Action 8.2

p99

Grammar in Action 8.3

p100

Everyday English 8.4

VOCABULARY
School

8.01 **1 Match the phrases with the photos (1–11). Then listen, check, and repeat.**

cheat on a test	☐	pass an exam	☐
fail an exam	☐	pay attention to the teacher	☐
get detention	☐	study for a test	☐
get good grades	☐	take an exam	☐
give somebody a talk	☐	write an essay	☐
hand in homework	1		

Pronunciation p142

8.04 **2 Listen and write the phrases you hear from Exercise 1. Then use the phrases to tell your partner what you remember.**

1 *get detention* 5 ______
2 ______ 6 ______
3 ______ 7 ______
4 ______ 8 ______

LEARN TO LEARN
Personalizing Vocabulary

Using new words to talk about your life helps you remember them.

3 Write true and false sentences about you with phrases from Exercise 1. Tell your partner your sentences. Can they guess which are false?

I always hand in my homework on time.

Use It!

4 Read the questions and write two more. Then ask and answer with a partner.

1 Is it better to study alone or with friends?
2 What should happen to students who cheat?
3 What are the good and bad things about exams?
______
______

Explore It!

Guess the correct answer.

How many students does the biggest school in the world have?

a between 25,000 and 35,000
b between 35,000 and 45,000
c more than 45,000

Find another interesting fact about a school. Then write a question for your partner to answer.

READING

A Report

1 **How many ways of getting to school can you think of?**

8.05 **2** **Read the report. Does it mention your ideas?**

3 **Match the headings (a–d) with the paragraphs (1–4).**

a A Suggestion for the Future
b Why Can't Every Child Go to School?
c A Risk, but an Essential One
d Introduction to My Report

4 **Circle the correct answers.**

1 What does the writer say about parents?
   a Their children shouldn't make dangerous journeys.
   b They care about their children's education.
   c They think it's difficult for children to get an education.
2 What does the writer think about online education?
   a It's more expensive than building bridges.
   b It could help more children learn.
   c It's a good idea if children have computers.

5 **Find words in the text that mean …**

1 looking for information (paragraph 1).

______

2 go regularly to a place (paragraph 2).

______

3 dangerous (paragraph 3).

______

Voice It!

6 **Discuss the statements.**

1 The children in the text are brave.
2 We need more online education for children.
3 Education is the most important thing for a happy, successful future.

Dangerous Journeys to School

1 ☐

This report looks at the problem of dangerous journeys to school. I have been researching this for my school project on education around the world. Here, I give some examples of these journeys and suggest one way to change the situation.

2 ☐

Children in many countries attend both elementary and secondary school. However, in some countries, school is too expensive or there aren't enough spots for everyone. In others, boys can go to school but girls can't. Some children aren't allowed to go to school because their parents need their help at home. In many cases, school is free and all children can attend, but some students make dangerous journeys to get there.

3 ☐

In Indonesia, for example, children from Batu Busuk village walk along a rope nine meters above a river and then walk 11 kilometers through a forest to get to school. They have been doing this since a bridge was destroyed in a rainstorm two years ago. In Los Pinos, Colombia, children cross the Rio Negro on an 800-meter rope because walking to school the long way takes four hours. In China, the children of Atuler village climb mountains to get to school. Children are allowed to make these risky journeys because education is important to parents and children everywhere.

4 ☐

Online education could be one answer to the problem. A teacher can give classes by video, and students can hand in homework by email and take exams online. Of course, electricity, a computer, and an internet connection are all necessary, but these things are cheaper to provide than roads and bridges. It is not a perfect solution, but if we spent money on these things, then children in remote places would have a basic education, and dangerous journeys to school would be a thing of the past.

Finished? p125 Ex. 1

GRAMMAR IN ACTION

Can/Can't

Watch video 8.2
What are boys not allowed to have in school?
What is Wu Yan allowed to do at school?

1 Complete the sentences with *can* or *can't*. Do they express permission, prohibition, or ability? Write *PE* (permission), *PR* (prohibition), or *A* (ability).

1. Students __can__ borrow two books from the library. (✓) __PE__
2. You ________ use a dictionary in the French exam. (✗) ________
3. Tom ________ play soccer very well. (✗) ________
4. Students ________ stay in the classroom when it's raining. (✓) ________
5. My sister ________ speak English better than me. (✓) ________

To Be Allowed To

+	The student **is allowed to** hand in homework by email.
-	Some children **aren't** [1] ____________ **to** go to school.
?	[2] ________ you **allowed to** take your phone to school? Yes, I **am**. No, I'**m** [3] ________.

2 Complete the examples in the chart above.

3 Rewrite the sentences with *to be allowed to*.

1. We can use a calculator in the exam.
   __We're allowed to use a calculator in the exam.__
2. My sister and I can't watch TV.
   ____
3. Can you choose the subjects you want to study?
   ____
4. Students at Luke's school can go home for lunch if they live near the school.
   ____

8.06 **4 Complete the text with the correct form of the words in the box. Then listen and check.**

can / come	~~can / play~~	can / wear
not allow / give	not allow / tell	not allow / wear

Every year, we have a big party on the last day of the school. We [1] __can play__ games or listen to music in class and the teachers [2] ____________ us any work! We [3] ____________ our own clothes instead of our uniform (although we [4] ____________ any jewelry – that's always against the rules). We [5] ____________ even ____________ in costumes if we want to. There's a competition for the best costume, but the teachers [6] ____________ us what the prize is – it's a surprise.

Use It!

5 Use the ideas to write questions with *to be allowed to* in your notebook.

have posters in your bedroom
~~play video games before dinner~~ stay out late
use your phone when you want

__Are you allowed to play video games before dinner?__

6 Ask and answer the questions in Exercise 5.

Are you allowed to play video games before dinner?

If I've finished all my homework.

Finished? p125 Ex. 2

VOCABULARY AND LISTENING

A Phone Call

1 Look at the photo. Why do you think the two students are cleaning the windows?

LEARN TO LEARN

Preparing to Listen

Deciding what you want to know about the topic before you listen helps you prepare.

2 You will hear Harry talking about his Japanese exchange trip. Write three questions you want to know the answer to.

____

____

____

8.07 3 Listen to the conversation. Then tell your partner which of your questions from Exercise 2 were answered.

8.07 4 Listen again and (circle) the correct answers.

1 How do Harry and Denise know each other?
   a They're brother and sister.   b They're friends.
2 When do the students clean the school?
   a in the morning   b at the end of the day
3 How well does Harry speak Japanese?
   a not at all   b not perfectly

Attitude and Behavior

8.08 5 Complete the chart with the opposite adjectives. Then listen, check, and repeat.

~~careful~~ ~~careless~~ disobedient disorganized immature mature organized polite rude well-behaved

Positive	Negative
careful	careless

6 Complete the school reports with the words from Exercise 5.

Andy used to be very [1] disobedient – never paying attention and always talking – but recently, I haven't had to give him a talk because he's been very [2] ____________. However, he's still very [3] ____________, especially with his books and papers. He should be more [4] ____________ and keep his things in order.

Last year, Lizzy was very [5] ____________ with her work and she made a lot of mistakes, but this year she has spent more time doing her homework and has been much more [6] ____________. She also used to be [7] ____________ and silly in class, always making jokes, but she has grown up a lot, and now she is much more [8] ____________.

Use It!

7 Put the words from Exercise 5 in order from most positive (1) to least positive (10). Then compare with a partner.

I think "polite" is the most positive because ...

GRAMMAR IN ACTION

To Have To, Must, and To Need To

Watch video 8.3
What don't the students have to carry with them? Why doesn't Anna need to study?

	To Have To	*Must*	*To Need To*
+	The students **have to** wear a uniform.	All students **must** attend orientation.	You **need to** make mistakes.
-	They **don't have to** do it.	Students **must not** (mustn't) use cell phones during the exam.	You **don't** [2] ________ tell me that.
?	**Do** you [1] ________ clean, too?		What [3] ________ we ________ do?

1 **Complete the examples in the chart above.**

2 **Complete the sentences with the correct form of *to have to*.**

1. You ~~don't have~~ to work in pairs. You can work alone if you want.
2. ________ you ________ wear a uniform?
3. Sam's teacher says she ________ study harder if she wants to pass her exams.
4. I ________ pay for guitar lessons. My best friend is teaching me!
5. ________ your parents ________ meet with your teachers once a year?

Get It Right!

The phrase **must not** means it's important not to do something. We use **don't have to** to express that an action is not necessary.

Visitors must not enter the school without permission

NOT ~~Visitors don't have to enter the school without permission.~~

3 **Rewrite the sentences with *to have to*, *must*, or *to need to*.**

1. It isn't necessary for us to wear a uniform.
   We don't need/have to wear a uniform.
2. It's obligatory for all students to take the exam.
   All students ________________.
3. Is it necessary for me to buy the book?
   Do I ________________?
4. It's against the rules for students to be late.
   Students ________________.
5. Joining an after-school club is optional. Students
   ________________.

4 **Write sentences about the signs with the phrases below and *to have to*, *must*, or *to need to*.**

be quiet ~~make an appointment~~
run wear formal clothes

1 Student Counselor's Office
Hours: 9:30 to 2:00
Monday to Friday
No appointment necessary

2 NO RUNNING IN THE HALLWAYS

3 Silence during the exam, please.

4 Graduation party:
July 23 at 6 p.m.
Formal clothes optional

1. You don't need/have to make an appointment.
2. ________________
3. ________________
4. ________________

Use It!

5 **Complete the rules for your dream school.**

1. We don't have to study ________________.
2. Teachers must not ________________.
3. We don't need to ________________.

6 EXAM **Ask and answer the questions with a partner.**

Student A:
What rules does your school have?
What would you change about your school's rules?

Student B:
What signs are in your school?
What rules do most people follow? What rules do they break?

Finished? p125 Ex. 3

SPEAKING

Explaining and Asking about Rules

8.09 **1 Listen to the conversation. How is Javier feeling about going on an exchange program?**

WILL	So, how are you feeling, Javier? Excited?
JAVIER	Kind of. I'm a little nervous, to be honest, Will.
WILL	Don't be. Everyone's really friendly and polite. But our rules might be a bit different from yours – for example, we have to wear a uniform, but that's no big deal. You'll love it!
JAVIER	Yeah, right! [1] What are the rules about phones?
WILL	You're not allowed to bring one to school.
JAVIER	How come? [2] ______________________
WILL	You get detention.
JAVIER	Really? In my school you're not allowed to use them in class, but we can use them during breaks. What about lunch? Do you have to eat in the cafeteria?
WILL	You don't have to. You can bring your own food if you want.
JAVIER	OK. [3] ______________________
WILL	Um, we have to wait outside the classroom for the teacher.
JAVIER	[4] ______________________
WILL	Because the teacher tells us where to sit as we go in the classroom.
JAVIER	It's a lot to remember.
WILL	Don't worry, you'll be fine!

8.09 **2 Complete the conversation with the phrases from the *Useful Language* box. Then listen again and check.**

Useful Language

Anything else I need to know?	~~What are the rules about … ?~~
What happens if you do?	Why's that?

3 Match the meanings (1–4) with the phrases in the *Everyday English* box.

1 A little bit.
2 Why?
3 I don't believe you!
4 That's not a big problem.

Watch video 8.4
Everyday English

How come?	☐	Kind of.	☐
That's no big deal.	☐	Yeah, right!	☐

PLAN

4 Plan your own conversation. Read the conversation in Exercise 1 again. Take notes about the three school rules Will and Javier talk about.

Phones: ______________________

Lunch: ______________________

Teachers: ______________________

5 Work in pairs. In your notebook, write notes on three rules in your school.

6 Plan a conversation to explain the rules to a friend from another country.

SPEAK

7 Practice a conversation. Remember to use *can/can't, to be allowed to, to have to, must, to need to,* and phrases from the *Useful Language* and *Everyday English* boxes.

CHECK

8 Work with another pair. Listen to their conversation. Which school rules did they talk about?

WRITING
An Essay

1 **Make a list of good and bad things about school uniforms. Then read the essay. Does it have your ideas?**

Should Students Have to Wear a Uniform?

For many students, a uniform is a part of daily life and they must wear it. But some students don't have to follow any rules about what to wear.
[1] ______________________ some advantages and disadvantages of uniforms.

People have strong views about uniforms. [2] ______________, wearing a uniform is preparation for the future. Many people have to wear one, such as firefighters, doctors, and nurses. [3] ______________ a uniform shows the world that you belong to an important group.

[4] ______________, you don't need to wear a uniform to get good grades. [5] ______________ youth is an important time to discover who you are. If students aren't allowed to be creative, they lose the opportunity to show their identity.

In summary, I think students should be able to choose what they wear. Uniforms are not necessary for success, and students might not have the freedom to be creative with their clothes when they start work.

2 **Put the parts of the essay in the correct order.**

- a a conclusion with the writer's opinion ☐
- b good things about school uniforms ☐
- c an introduction to the topic ☐
- d bad things about school uniforms ☐

3 **Complete the essay with the phrases from the *Useful Language* box.**

Useful Language

In this essay, I outline …
On the other hand, …
Some say that …
On the one hand, …
Others argue that …

PLAN

4 **Write your own essay. Think of two good things and two bad things about using phones in schools. Write notes.**

Good Things: ______________________

____

Bad Things: ______________________

____

5 **Look at the essay question below. Write notes on your opinion. Decide what to include. Use the information in Exercise 2 to help you.**

Can phones help students learn in class?

____

____

____

WRITE

6 **Write your essay. Remember to include *can/can't*, *to be allowed to*, *to have to*, *must*, *to need to*, and the phrases from the *Useful Language* box.**

CHECK

7 **Do you …**

- have an introduction and conclusion?
- write about good things and bad things?

Finished? p125 Ex. 4

CITIZENSHIP PROJECT

A School Brochure

1 **Read the brochure for Unity Hill School. What is special about this school?**

2 **Write down the things you like and don't like about Unity Hill. Then compare your answers.**

I like that every student can suggest a new rule, and every student has the right to vote on it.

How to Make Decisions in a Group

8.10 **3** **Put the stages of decision-making in order. Then listen to the students from Unity Hill. Do they follow the same order?**

- a Find the best solution. ☐
- b Check the group is ready to vote. ☐
- c Present the problem. 1
- d Vote on the decision. ☐
- e Ask for suggestions. ☐
- f Discuss the pros and cons of each idea. ☐

Unity Hill School

Introduction

Are you organized? Do you want to get good grades and develop skills to succeed in our modern world? Then come to Unity Hill – one of the most exciting schools of the 21st century.

What Makes Unity Hill Unique?

We believe our students should be responsible for their school, so at Unity Hill the students make the rules. Every student can suggest a new rule, and every student can vote on it.

Rules Students Have Decided

- Students must respect other students and staff.
- Students don't have to wear a uniform. However, if students decide to have a uniform in the future, they will design it.
- Students have to study seven subjects, but they can choose which ones. One of the subjects must be a language.
- Students have to do PE twice a week, but they don't have to do the same sport every time.
- Students must not use their phones in class, but they can use them during lunch.
- Students don't have to do homework on the weekend.

Responsibilities

- Students can vote yes or no on new rules, but after a new rule has been decided, students must follow it, even if they voted no.
- Students can use any of the facilities, but they have to keep everything clean.
- Students don't have to eat the school lunch, but if they do, they have to help clean up.

PLAN

4 Work in groups to design a school brochure. Complete the steps.

- Decide why your school is special.
- Choose a school name.
- Suggest some school rules.
- Discuss and vote on the rules.
- Decide what responsibilities students will have.
- Decide who prepares each part of the brochure.

PRESENT

5 Present your brochure to the class. Remember to include an introduction and explain why your school is special, the rules, and the responsibilities.

CHECK

6 Read your classmates' brochures. What rules do they have? Which school do you like?

8 REVIEW

VOCABULARY

1 Complete the text.

cheat on tests · grades · pass · studied · take

Sometimes I used to [1] ______________ by copying my classmates because I hadn't [2] ______________ at all. These days I'm different. Next year I have to [3] ______________ some important exams and I really want to [4] ______________ them and get good [5] ______________.

2 Write two adjectives to describe each student.

careful · disobedient · immature · organized · polite · rude

1 Sometimes Lilly is silly in class and says bad things to her classmates.

____

____

2 Gareth speaks nicely to everyone and plans his work well.

____

____

3 Ben behaves very badly at school, but he pays a lot of attention to his homework.

____

____

GRAMMAR IN ACTION

3 Complete the texts with the correct form of *to be allowed to* and the verbs in the box.

bring · study · use

EduTV

Should students [1] ______________ the subjects they want? We want to hear from you for our new documentary: *Should We Choose Our Education?*

Home · Inbox · Sent · New

Dear Parents,

We are writing to remind you that students [2] ______________ their phones to school, but they [3] ______________ them in class. Please do not call students during classes.

Sincerely,

The Principal

4 Circle the correct options.

1 Ben *needs to / doesn't have to / must not* study Spanish if he doesn't want to. He can choose Arabic instead.
2 Students *need to / don't have to / must not* play games on school computers.
3 We *need to / don't have to / must not* wear a uniform at school. We can wear what we want.
4 Toni *needs to / doesn't have to / must not* pay more attention in class – she never listens!

Self-Assessment

I can talk about school in English.

I can talk about attitude and behavior.

I can use *can/can't* and *to be allowed to*.

I can use *to have to*, *must*, and *to need to*.

LEARN TO ... ASK FOR HELP WHEN YOU DON'T UNDERSTAND

There are different ways to ask English speakers for help and check if you understand what they've said.

1 Have you ever had any of these problems? How did you solve them?

Problems Understanding Someone in English

a The other person speaks too fast.
b The person uses a lot of words I don't know.
c I understand, more or less, but I don't understand all of the details.
d I think I understand, but I'm not 100 percent sure.
e I'm too shy to say that I don't understand.

2 Match situations a–d with conversations 1–4.

a ☐ explaining the rules of a game
b ☐ at the train station
c ☐ asking directions
d ☐ studying in class

1
A OK, everybody, why are infographics useful online?
B Teacher, [1]___.
A Which word? Infographic?
B Yes.
A OK, an infographic is ...

2
A If you land on a blue square, you have to take a card, but you must not show it to anyone. But if you ...
B [2]___. I don't understand very well.
A Sorry! I always speak too fast when I'm excited. OK, if you land ...

3
A Excuse me, how do I get to the museum?
B Go straight down this road, cross the bridge, and it's on the corner.
A Sorry. [3]___.
B Sure, go straight down this road, cross the bridge, ...

4
A Excuse me, I'm trying to get to the airport.
B You need to take the blue line to Airport Station. Then from the station take the shuttle bus.
A OK, [4]___. I take the blue line to Airport Station?
B That's right.
A And then the shuttle bus?
B Exactly.
A Thanks.

3 Complete the conversations in Exercise 2 with these phrases. Write a–d in the gaps.

a Could you speak more slowly, please
b I don't understand what that word means
c Let me check I've got this right
d Could you say that again, please

SHAPE IT!

4 Work in pairs. Take turns talking about one of the topics below. Use the phrases in Exercise 3 to help you understand.

how to get from your school to your house
how to make and use the past perfect
how to use a social media app
the rules of a club you are in
the rules of a sport

9 Where would you go?

LEARNING OUTCOMES

I can ...

- understand texts about vacations in the future and vacation situations
- talk about a future trip
- write an email
- use *to be going to*, the present continuous, the future continuous, relative pronouns, and relative clauses
- talk about travel and use phrasal verbs
- make verb and noun collocations, record phrasal verbs by preposition, make adjectives from nouns, and use technology to practice English

Start It!

1 Look at the photo. Would you like to be in this place? Why / Why not?
2 Before you watch, do you think we'll be able to go to the moon on vacation soon?
3 How long is a day on the moon? Watch and check.
4 Would you like to go to space? Why / Why not?

Watch video 9.1

p109

Grammar in Action 9.2

p111

Grammar in Action 9.3

p112

Everyday English 9.4

p114

Globetrotters 9.5

1

2

3

4

5

6

7

8

VOCABULARY

Travel

9.01 **1 Match the words with the photos (1–8) and definitions (9–12). Then listen, check, and repeat.**

abroad	☐	journey	☐
accommodation	1	resort	☐
backpacking	☐	sightseeing	☐
book	☐	tour	☐
cruise ship	☐	tourist attraction	☐
destination	☐	trip	☐

9 a visit to and around a place, often with a guide
10 in or to a foreign country
11 a (usually short) visit to another place
12 the act of traveling to a place (usually long distance)

Pronunciation p142

9.04 **2 Listen and circle the correct words.**

1 *trip / accommodation*
2 *tourist attraction / cruise ship*
3 *tour / abroad*
4 *book / backpacking*
5 *destination / journey*

LEARN TO LEARN

Learning Collocations

When you learn new words, write which verbs they can be used with.

3 Complete the chart with words from Exercise 1. Add *a* if necessary.

Go	abroad, ______, ______
Book	______, ______, ______
Go on	______, ______, ______, ______
Visit	______, ______
Arrive at	______, ______

Use It!

4 In your notebook, write questions with the collocations from Exercise 3 and the ideas in the box.

Have you ever … ?
When was the last time you … ?
Do you like … ? Would you like to … ?

Have you ever been on a cruise ship?

5 Ask and answer your questions from Exercise 4.

Have you ever been on a cruise ship?

Yes, I went on a cruise ship around the Caribbean last year.

Explore It!

Guess the correct answer.

Which country has the most tourists each year?

a the U.S.A. b Spain c France

Find another interesting fact about a tourist destination. Then write a question for your partner to answer.

READING

A Magazine Interview

1 **Look at the picture. How do you think vacations will be different in 2030?**

9.05 2 **Read the magazine interview. Does it mention any of your ideas?**

3 EXAM **Complete the interview with the sentences. There are three extra sentences.**

A No, or on trains, in hotels, or at tourist attractions either.
B Tourists will travel by robot horse.
C The trip used to take six hours.
~~D One of the main changes will be where people go on vacation.~~
E People will go on many more vacations.
F Space tourism will be a lot of fun.
G More passengers will be traveling by high-speed train than by plane.
H Mars will be a favorite tourist resort.

4 **Complete the chart with words from the interview.**

Noun	Adjective Form
[1] ______ or tourist	touristy
adventure	[2] ______
smell	[3] ______
pilot	[4] ______

Voice It!

5 **Discuss the questions.**

1 Do you agree with Chen's predictions? Why / Why not?
2 What surprises you most about vacations in the future?
3 Which vacation from the interview would you most like to go on? Why?

VACATIONS OF THE FUTURE

Katya What is going to be the biggest change in tourism in the future?

Chen [1] D . In 2030, for example, we won't be staying at campsites. People will be sleeping in far more exciting accommodations, like floating resorts and hotels under the sea. Imagine waking up face-to-face with a shark! And if that's not adventurous enough, how about relaxing at a space hotel in zero gravity and going on day trips to the moon? [2]___. However, it might be a little smelly, as space tourists won't be able to take a shower!

Katya Ugh! So, in 2030, will tourists still be traveling to the same destinations as now?

Chen Yes, they will, but they'll be using virtual reality to test them first. Tourists will be able to experience resorts before they book their trip to help them choose the perfect destination.

Katya And how will tourists travel there?

Chen Good question. We won't be teleporting for a while, but some experts predict that the way people travel will change. [3]___. Next week, I'm traveling from Beijing to Shanghai by high-speed train in just four and a half hours, and that journey is predicted to get even shorter in the future. [4]___. Airplanes aren't going to disappear, but the whole flying experience is going to change. Flights will be quicker, and by 2040, passengers will even be flying on pilotless planes, looking up at the sky through a clear roof while enjoying a meal served by a robot.

Katya So, won't there be any humans working on planes?

Chen [5]___.

Finished? p126 Ex. 1

GRAMMAR IN ACTION

To Be Going To and Present Continuous for Future

Watch video 9.2
What does Matt predict he'll be doing by 2022?
What will everybody be doing this summer?

The whole flying experience **is going to change**.
Next week **I'm traveling** from Beijing to Shanghai.

1 Look at the examples above and complete the sentences with *to be going to* or the present continuous. Use the verbs in parentheses. Which are arrangements? Which are predictions?

1 Next week I'm going (go) to Turkey on vacation. arrangement
2 Technology ______ (change) our ideas about space tourism. ______
3 Robots ______ (do) more jobs on planes and in hotels. ______
4 Tomorrow I ______ (travel) to Istanbul by high-speed train. ______
5 We ______ (meet) her at the airport two hours before the flight departs. ______

Use It!

2 In your notebook, write three arrangements and three predictions about next weekend with *to be going to* and the present continuous.

I'm having lunch with my friends on Saturday.
I'm going to have a great time with my friends.

Future Continuous

+	By 2040, passengers [1] will even **be flying** on pilotless planes.
–	In 2030, we [2] ______ **be staying** at campsites.
?	In 2030, **will** tourists still [3] ______ to the same destinations as now? Yes, they [4] ______ . / No, they **won't**.

3 Complete the examples in the chart above. Use the magazine interview on page 108 to help you.

4 In your notebook, write sentences in the future continuous.

1 In the future, tourists / stay / on the moon
In the future, tourists will be staying on the moon.
2 By this time next week I / camp / in Greece
3 Where / you / live / when you're 30 / ?
4 Humans / not work / in hotels in the future

9.06 **5 Circle the correct options to complete the conversation. Then listen and check.**

KATYA Look at this article! It says that soon passports [1] *are going to disappear* / *are disappearing*! By 2030, we [2] *aren't showing* / *won't be showing* passports to people at the airport; robots [3] *will be checking* / *are checking* people's identity instead.

FABIO Yeah, technology [4] *'s going to change* / *'s changing* everything in the future. I think it [5] *'s going to make* / *'ll be making* everything quicker and safer.

KATYA I guess so, but in a few years' time, robots [6] *are doing* / *will be doing* most jobs, so there [7] *aren't being* / *aren't going to be* any jobs for us!

FABIO Ha ha! We [8] *'ll be sitting* / *'re sitting* at home while the robots do all the work!

Use It!

6 In your notebook, write predictions about vacations and travel in the future.

By 2050, we'll be traveling by air taxi.

Finished? p126 Ex. 2

VOCABULARY AND LISTENING

Travel Phrasal Verbs

9.07 **1 Match the phrasal verbs with the underlined phrases and then write the correct form of the phrasal verbs. Listen, check, and repeat.**

check in check out get away get back get in ~~go away~~ look around set off take off

1 go away 4 ______ 7 ______
2 ______ 5 ______ 8 ______
3 ______ 6 ______ 9 ______

Hello!
We're on vacation! Dad said he wanted to [1]leave on vacation because he was stressed and that now would be a great time to [2]escape somewhere, so we booked it!
We haven't had time to [3]explore yet because we didn't [4]arrive until 8 p.m. Our plane was delayed, so we didn't [5]start flying until 2:30 p.m.! We [6]started our journey at 6 a.m., so we're all really tired. We've just [7]arrived at the hotel and we're going out to dinner in a minute.
We have to [8]leave the hotel by noon next Friday, so we'll [9]come home at about 9 p.m.
See you then!

Lauren Rogers
15 Castle Street
Newcastle, WA 98056

LEARN TO LEARN

Phrasal Verbs

When you learn a new phrasal verb, write it down with other phrasal verbs that have the same preposition.

2 Complete the chart with the phrasal verbs from Exercise 1.

around	away	back	in	off	out
look					

Use It!

3 Complete the questions with the phrasal verbs from Exercise 1. Then ask and answer the questions with a partner.

1 When was the last time you went away?
2 What documents do you need when you ______ in at a hotel or airport?
3 Do you enjoy looking ______ new places?
4 What time do you usually ______ off in the morning?
5 How do you feel when you get ______ from a vacation?
6 What time did you ______ in last night?

I went away to Peru last summer with my parents.

Conversations

9.08 **4 Listen and match the conversations (1–4) with the photos (a–d).**

a ☐

b ☐

c ☐

d ☐

9.08 **5 Listen again. Are the sentences *T* (true) or *F* (false)?**

1 Alfie prefers his dad's vacation plans. ___
2 Peter wanted to set off earlier. ___
3 Isla would like to go on a trip to space. ___
4 Tim doesn't believe there will be floating hotels in the future. ___

Voice It!

6 Discuss the questions.

1 What's your favorite type of vacation? Why?
2 Would you fly on a plane with a robot pilot?

Watch video 9.3
Name one place where she wants to go one day. At what point in the future does she imagine she travels to?

GRAMMAR IN ACTION

Relative Pronouns and Relative Clauses

Person	She's the type of person **who** just wants to spend her vacation swimming.
Thing	It's a system [1] that uses virtual reality.
Place	Dad wants to go to a place [2] ________ he can go sightseeing.
Time	We already live in a time [3] ________ people want to go away on exciting vacations.
Reason	This is [4] ________ I told you we needed to set off earlier.
Possession	The girl in our class **whose** dad works for a technology company …

1 **Complete the examples in the chart above.**

2 **Circle the correct words.**

1. The tent *that* / *whose* I bought is broken!
2. I'm the person *whose* / *who* sent you the message.
3. That's the boy *whose* / *who* grandparents went on vacation to Greece.
4. July is the month *when* / *who* most people go on vacation.
5. Jon is very confident. That's *why* / *when* he's so good at languages.
6. A destination is the place *when* / *where* you travel to.

3 **Complete the text. Then listen and check.** 9.09

The other day I met a guy [1] whose cousin is training to be an astronaut. He told me that the place [2] ________ she is training is looking for people [3] ________ want to go into space as tourists and she is going to go. She says the reason [4] ________ she wants to go is to show people that space travel is something [5] ________ anyone can do if they complete the training. She's not sure [6] ________ she is leaving, but the training [7] ________ she has done so far means she is ready to set off any day now!

Get It Right!

The relative pronoun replaces the subject pronoun in a relative clause.

A vacation that ~~it~~ cost $500.

The tourists who ~~they~~ are staying in my hotel.

4 **Circle the correct words. Then complete the sentences with your own ideas.**

1. My favorite vacation destination is a place *who* / *where* I can go skiing.
2. I prefer to stay in accommodations *that* / *when* ________________.
3. A friend is someone *who* / *why* ________________.
4. School is the reason *where* / *why* ________________.
5. My favorite store is the one *that* / *when* ________________.

Use It!

5 **Think of two words for each of the categories in the box. Then write a sentence with a relative clause to describe each word in your notebook.**

animals	famous people	places	things

Paris: It's a place where you can see the Eiffel Tower.

Finished? p126 Ex. 3

SPEAKING

Talking About a Future Trip

9.10 **1 Listen to the conversation. What is Gemma going to do on her trip?**

BEN Hey Gemma! So, when are you off to New York?

GEMMA Hey, Ben! Hang on a sec. I'll be with you in a minute. Hey, Sandy. I'll talk to you later. Bye. Sorry, that was my sister on the phone. What were you saying?

BEN I was asking you when you're going to New York.

GEMMA We're going [1] *in two weeks*. I can't wait!

BEN I'm so jealous! New York's on my bucket list. [2] ____________________

GEMMA We're staying in a hotel. It's right in the middle of Manhattan!

BEN Wow! And [3] ____________________

GEMMA Oh, you know, all the usual stuff, so tons of sightseeing. [4] ____________________ seeing the Empire State Building, Statue of Liberty, Times Square, and so on. [5] ____________________ get tickets to see a show. Mom wants to see *The Lion King*, but I'd rather see *Hamilton*.

BEN [6] ____________________

GEMMA Just a week.

BEN It's not fair! While you're jetting off to New York, think of us back home. We'll all be studying for our exams!

GEMMA Ah, poor you! I'll send you some photos!

9.10 **2 Complete the conversation with the phrases from the *Useful Language* box. Then listen again and check.**

Useful Language

How long are you going for?
I'm really looking forward to (+ *-ing*)
~~… in two weeks~~
We're going to try to …
What are you planning on doing?
Where will you be staying?

3 Match the meanings (1–5) with the phrases in the *Everyday English* box.

1 exactly in the center of
2 What were you talking about?
3 together with other similar things
4 list of things to do before you die
5 things

Watch video 9.4 Everyday English

… and so on	☐	bucket list	☐
… right in the middle of …	☐	the usual stuff	☐
What were you saying?	☐		

PLAN

4 Read the conversation in Exercise 1 again. Write notes about Gemma's plans.

Going where? ____________________
When? ____________________
Staying where? ____________________
____
Going to do what? ____________________
____

5 Work in pairs. Plan a conversation about visiting a place. Use the ideas from Exercise 4.

SPEAK

6 Practice a conversation. Remember to use *to be going to*, the present continuous, the future continuous, relative pronouns, and phrases from the *Useful Language* and *Everyday English* boxes.

CHECK

7 Work with another pair. Listen to their conversation and answer the questions from Exercise 4.

WRITING
An Email to a Host Family

1 **Look at the photo. Where is it? Why do you think Kerem is going there? Read his email and check.**

From: kerem29@mymail.com
Subject: Next month

Dear Mr. and Mrs. O'Reilly,

I'm writing to introduce myself, as I'm coming to stay with you in San Francisco next month. My name is Kerem. I'm 14 years old and I'm from Bursa in Turkey. Do you know Turkey?

I'm very excited about visiting San Francisco. It'll be my first visit to the United States, so I wanted to ask you some questions about my trip. My friends and I are taking a bus from the airport. Is someone going to meet us there when we arrive? Also, do you know how many hours of English we will be studying every day? I know we'll be sightseeing in the afternoons, but do you know which places we'll be visiting? What's the weather going to be like? What clothes do you think I should bring?

Thank you very much for inviting me to stay with you. I'm really looking forward to meeting you!

Best wishes,

Kerem

2 **Put a–e in the order they appear in Kerem's email.**

a ☐ goodbye
b ☐ questions about the trip
c ☐ greeting
d ☐ reason for writing
e ☐ thanks

3 **Match the phrases from Exercise 2 (a–e) with the phrases in the *Useful Language* box.**

Useful Language

Best wishes, ☐
Dear Mr. and Mrs. … ☐
Do you know … ? ☐
I'm writing to … ☐
Thank you very much for (+ *-ing*) ☐

PLAN

4 **Write your own email to a host family. Think of questions to ask them about these things.**

Your Travel Plans and When You Arrive

____

____

Activities While You are There

____

____

The Weather and Clothes to Bring

____

____

5 **Decide what information to include. Use the information in Exercise 2 to help you.**

WRITE

6 **Write your email. Remember to use *to be going to*, the present continuous, the future continuous, and phrases from the *Useful Language* box.**

CHECK

7 **Do you …**

- use a greeting at the beginning and say goodbye at the end?
- say why you are writing?
- say thank you?

Finished? p126 Ex. 4

AROUND THE WORLD

READING
A Webpage

1 Look at the photos. What do you know about Costa Rica? Discuss with a partner.

2 (9.11) Read the webpage. Does it mention any of your ideas?

Globetrotters

Watch video 9.5
One World, One Culture?

- What makes culture? Think of three things.
- How many H&M shops are there around the world?
- What are the advantages and disadvantages of a global culture?

Costa Rica

Volunteer Abroad Conservation Programs

1 Why visit Costa Rica?

Costa Rica is a fascinating, tropical country in Central America. It is also one of the happiest countries in the world because of its relaxed way of life. When you ask someone "How are you?" they answer "pura vida." That means "pure life" or "life is great." Although it's only a small country, it is home to 5 percent of the world's plant and animal species! Over 25 percent of the country is protected, as it is made up of **outstanding** nature reserves. Here you can find more than 1,000 butterflies, 9,000 different types of plants, 20,000 species of spider, and 34,000 varieties of insects! Costa Rica has **spectacular** volcanoes, beaches, jungles, rainforests, and magical cloud forests!

2 Why is conservation so important in Costa Rica?

It's a destination that has always been popular for tourism, and many tourists go back year after year. In fact, tourism is the main reason why conservation is so important. Costa Ricans are proud of their country and they work hard to take care of its **unique** natural beauty. Ecotourism in Costa Rica helps protect the natural environment, benefit local communities, and also educate tourists about the importance of its natural resources.

3 What will I be doing?

Volunteers stay in a coastal town and work on environmental projects. You'll be keeping the beaches clean and safe to protect turtle eggs, and you'll count the baby turtles before they return to the ocean. You'll be helping with wildlife research and will also be working on community projects where you'll be doing some gardening, as well as helping build schools and community centers.

4 Am I going to have any free time?

Yes, you'll be able to get away in your free time to go sightseeing or on day trips to the capital, San José. You can also look around the **stunning** Tortuguero or Manuel Antonio national parks.

What better way to see and explore Costa Rica while making a difference for the local wildlife! So, what are you waiting for? Volunteer now and make a difference!

3 Write the adjectives in **bold** that describe Costa Rica's ...

1 nature reserves. ____________
2 geographical features. ____________
3 natural beauty. ____________
4 national parks. ____________

Voice It!

4 **Discuss the questions.**

1 Why is volunteering and helping others important?
2 Volunteering is one way to make a difference in the world around you. How do people volunteer in your country?
3 How can you make a difference in your everyday life?

LEARN TO LEARN

Making Adjectives from Nouns

When you read a text, try to find different forms of words you already know.

5 **Find adjectives in the webpage for the nouns (1–6).**

1 tropics tropical
2 center ____________
3 magic ____________
4 nature ____________
5 coast ____________
6 environment ____________

Explore It!

Guess the correct answer.

Costa Ricans have at least 12 different words for ...

a rain. b butterflies. c volcanoes.

Find another interesting fact about Costa Rica. Then write a question for your partner to answer.

SHAPE IT!

CULTURE PROJECT

A Poster

A poster gives information about a topic in an attractive visual way. In groups, make a poster about a volunteer program.

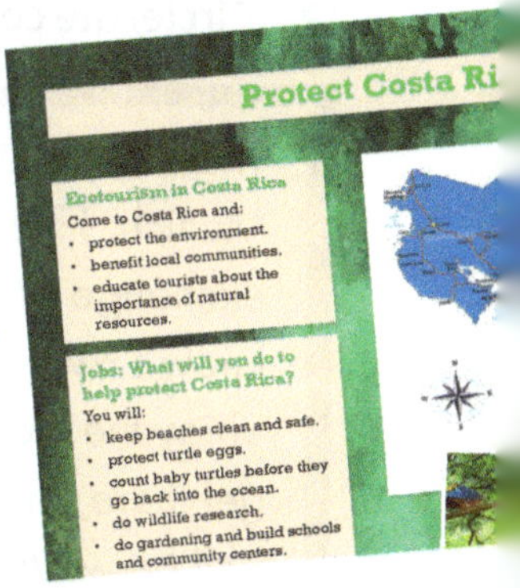

Teacher's Resource Bank

9 REVIEW

VOCABULARY

1 Complete the text with the words in the box.

abroad accommodation backpacking cruise ship destination journey resort tourist attractions

Going on a [1]__________ is exciting, especially if you're going [2]__________ to explore another country, but there's a lot to do before you go. First, you need to decide where to go: a popular [3]__________ with a hotel and pool or a less well-known [4]__________ with fewer tourists? Then there's the [5]__________ to think about. Are you going to stay in a hotel or an apartment? Or perhaps you prefer to go [6]______________ around several cities, visiting all the famous [7]__________ or sailing to different places on a [8]__________. Whatever you decide, enjoy it!

2 Add prepositions to the sentences.

1 It's too hot in my town in the summer, so we like to get ________. We usually go to the beach.
2 Let's set ________ at 9 a.m. Then we can check ________ to the hotel and take a look ________ the city.
3 What time does your flight get ________? I'll come and meet you at the airport.

GRAMMAR IN ACTION

3 Circle the correct form of the verbs.

This time next week, I [1]*fly* / *'ll be flying* to Munich. I [2]*'m going* / *'ll be going* on a school exchange program, but I'm a little nervous. I know I [3]*won't be enjoying* / *'m not going to enjoy* the flight because I hate flying. When we get there, our host families [4]*are waiting* / *will be waiting* for us at the airport. I think I [5]*'ll be missing* / *'m going to miss* my friends.

4 Complete the text with relative pronouns.

The reason [1]________ many big tourist destinations are next to the ocean is because the ocean provides food. Nowadays, many are overcrowded, and we need to find new places [2]________ people can stay. One solution is to build resorts [3]________ float on the water. In the future, people will make big floating areas [4]________ will support hotels, campsites, and other accommodations. In summer, [5]________ it gets hot, the floating areas will move further out to sea to keep the city cool.

Self-Assessment

I can talk about travel in English.	☹	😐	☺
I can use travel phrasal verbs.	☹	😐	☺
I can use *to be going to* and the present continuous for future.	☹	😐	☺
I can use the future continuous.	☹	😐	☺
I can use relative pronouns and relative clauses.	☹	😐	☺

LEARN TO ... USE TECHNOLOGY TO PRACTICE ENGLISH

When you learn a language, it's important to practice as much as possible. Technology can help you do that.

1 **Read what two students say about using technology to practice English. Then complete the chart with *G* (Gorka), *A* (Amanda), or *B* (both).**

GORKA

I downloaded a free flash card app for learning vocabulary. You can make your own flash cards and test yourself. Also, I've just changed my phone language and all my social media apps to English. Now I see and read English hundreds of times a day! I also listen to podcasts in English about sports, usually when I'm on the bus to school. I need to start watching videos online as well – my friends tell me that's a great way to learn.

AMANDA

I read a lot of books in English, so I have a dictionary app on my phone to look up new words. Also, there are thousands of videos online for practicing English. Some of them are really funny, and they're free, too! I like to watch them on my phone. What else? Well, once a week I have a video call with my cousin Kylie in Sydney. She doesn't speak any Turkish, so the conversation has to be in English! I really should change my social apps to English, too.

Ways to Use Technology to Practice English	Who Does This?
1 use your phone to practice English	B
2 use an app for learning vocabulary	
3 watch videos in English	
4 listen to podcasts in English	
5 speak face-to-face online with an English speaker	
6 have English as your phone language	
7 have English as the language of your social media	

2 **Ask and answer the questions about each of the ways to use technology in Exercise 1.**

1 Have you tried this? How easy or difficult was it? How useful was it?

2 If you haven't tried this, would you like to? Why / Why not?

3 **Which three ways of using technology to practice English are the most useful? Explain your reasons.**

I think podcasts are really useful because you can find ones about a lot of different topics, and it's important to practice listening.

That's true, but I think changing your phone language to English would be more useful because you use your phone all the time.

SHAPE IT!

4 **Complete the action plan with three ways to use technology to practice English. Tell your partner. Do you have similar plans?**

My action plan for using technology to practice English. I'm going to ...
1
2
3

What are you going to do?

I'm going to download a flash card app to learn and practice new vocabulary.

Good idea. I'm going to ...

5 FINISHED?

1 Circle five more words about planet Earth in the wordsearch.

P	T	O	X	Y	G	E	N
O	H	G	U	T	I	W	Z
L	E	K	Y	U	O	I	W
L	P	Y	S	Y	T	L	A
U	L	I	F	E	O	D	S
T	A	L	G	W	P	L	T
I	N	A	H	E	D	I	E
O	E	Q	J	S	N	F	E
N	T	P	G	H	J	E	R
E	E	N	E	R	G	Y	Q

2 Match the sentence strips to make six first conditional sentences.

If you go for a walk in the winter,

unless you eat healthy food.

If you go out at night,

You could get sick very quickly

you may be lucky enough to see bats flying.

if they go out in the rain.

They will get wet

I might go for a walk on the beach.

you could fall on some ice.

unless they go on an organized tour.

Tourists cannot go into the castle

If I have time tomorrow,

3 Complete the story with the missing phrases.

If I had a time machine, I [1]___. If I could do that, I [2]___ when we invented plastic. If I did that, I [3]___. If that happened, we [4]___. If we didn't have that, [5]___. If it was cleaner, [6]___ and people would be happier. But there's a problem! If we didn't have plastic, we [7]___ or bottles or pens or anything! If we didn't have all these things, our lives [8]___. So maybe I wouldn't go back in time! But, wouldn't the world be [9]___ if everyone recycled their waste?

a wouldn't have plastic waste
b could travel back in time
c there would be more animals
d would be very difficult
e would like to travel to the time
f the world would be cleaner
g would stop people from creating plastic
h wouldn't have computers
i a better place

4 Write the letters in the correct order to make words to complete the sentences.

1 You can find sea birds, seals, and crabs on the TSCOA. coast
2 You might see a polar bear standing on an BRGEEIC. ________
3 You can find fish in a MRTEAS. ________
4 Bears sometimes live in a VCEA. ________
5 A lot of different animals live in a TEARSFINRO. ________
6 There are butterflies living in the LLYEVA near where I live. ________

6 FINISHED?

1 **Complete the crossword.**

Across

4 make a liquid move from one place to another
5 make something larger in amount or size
8 heat a liquid to a very high temperature
9 join something to something else
11 make something less

Down

1 put something over something else
2 make something very, very cold
3 move a liquid with a spoon
6 take something away
7 put something in a particular position
10 push something
12 put something into a liquid for a short time

2 **Read the riddles. What are the objects?**

1 *What am I? I am made of glass and metal, plastic, or wood. I am put on the wall or on a shelf. I am looked at by many people. A picture is placed inside me. I am made in different sizes.*
I am a ______________________.

2 *What am I? I am made of wood, metal, or plastic. I am found in the kitchen. I am used to stir liquids.*
I am a ______________________.

3 **Do the quiz. Guess and circle the answers.**

1 When was the first TV program shown?
a 1910 b 1928 c 1935 d 1950

2 When was the first email sent?
a 1971 b 1983 c 1990 d 2001

3 When was the first car invented?
a 1798 b 1832 c 1885 d 1901

4 When was the first chocolate bar made?
a 1655 b 1847 c 1922 d 1940

5 When was the first supermarket opened?
a 1850 b 1900 c 1910 d 1930

6 When was the first smartphone sold?
a 1994 b 1997 c 2010 d 2007

4 **Complete the lists.**

Things in my house made out of:

- cardboard: *boxes* ______________________.
- glass: ______________________
- leather: ______________________
- rubber: ______________________
- silk: ______________________
- tin: ______________________

Things in my house kept in a:

- bag: ______________________
- box: ______________________
- can: ______________________
- case: ______________________
- jar: ______________________
- tube: ______________________

7 FINISHED?

1 Circle 11 more festival words in the wordsearch.

F	G	P	M	T	C	L	K	D	E	A	E
G	I	G	R	R	V	H	L	R	S	M	P
P	X	R	O	O	F	S	E	A	U	F	C
A	E	W	E	W	G	H	T	T	J	A	E
R	D	K	N	W	P	R	S	A	S	I	R
A	Q	T	L	S	O	O	A	A	L	R	E
D	R	R	O	S	C	R	L	M	X	L	M
E	V	M	Z	Q	G	G	K	Q	H	E	O
I	T	F	L	O	A	T	A	S	F	B	N
A	D	E	C	O	R	A	T	I	O	N	Y
L	A	N	T	E	R	N	T	W	W	U	P
D	O	P	F	R	A	Z	Q	W	P	H	T

2 What had you done by 9 p.m. yesterday? Write as many things as you can remember.

By 9 p.m. yesterday, I'd done all my homework, I'd cleaned my room, I'd read 100 pages of a book, I'd watched a parade, I'd been to a festival …

3 Guess who said the following. Then rewrite the sentences as reported speech in your notebook.

bass player ~~country music singer~~ jazz musician

1 We are a successful local act, but we hope to play at a big country music festival one day. We want to perform in front of an international audience.

country music singer: The country music singer said they were a …

2 We are going to play all our latest songs as well as our greatest hits at the event. We hope to sell a lot of albums.

3 We've received an invitation to open the concert for a famous jazz singer on her next European tour. We are going to play at a new concert hall in Spain.

4 Write the letters in the correct order to make words connected to music festivals and live music.

1 igg
2 ndab smeebmr
3 akcrt
4 inpospurtg tac
5 lenirehad
6 nett
7 ectamips
8 etasg
9 uneev
10 recone

8 FINISHED?

1 **Circle nine more verbs in the wordsearch. Then use the verbs to complete the phrases about school.**

Q	E	S	V	S	A	O	H	R	S
G	E	T	H	T	W	H	G	M	T
D	A	W	T	U	A	R	R	T	R
E	F	D	I	D	Y	C	I	Z	L
P	A	Y	V	Y	P	I	S	T	L
T	I	H	J	K	E	D	P	P	E
A	L	B	B	C	H	E	A	T	S
F	T	A	L	K	Q	U	S	M	O
H	A	N	D	D	E	C	S	A	E
E	S	P	N	T	A	K	E	M	Q

1 ___cheat___ on a test
2 ________ / ________ / ________ an exam
3 ________ good grades
4 give somebody a ________
5 ________ in homework
6 ________ attention to the teacher
7 ________ for a test
8 ________ an essay

2 **Read the clues and answer the questions.**

1 You can whisper, but you can't shout. You can take things, but you aren't allowed to keep them. Where am I? ___in a library___
2 You can have fun, but you aren't allowed to stand. You can go with your friends, but you aren't allowed to talk to them. Where am I? ________________
3 You can exercise here, but you can't walk or run. Where am I? ________________
4 You can buy it and wear it. But you aren't allowed to change it. What is it? ________________
5 You can sit with a lot of other students, but you aren't allowed to work with them. What am I? ________________

3 **Invent a sport and its rules. Use *to have to*, *to need to*, and *must* and words from the box.**

ball bat captain catch court field game goal half-time hit kick lose loser net pass player pool team throw point win winner

____
____
____

4 **Four pairs of friends are complete opposites. Follow the lines and match the three other pairs.**

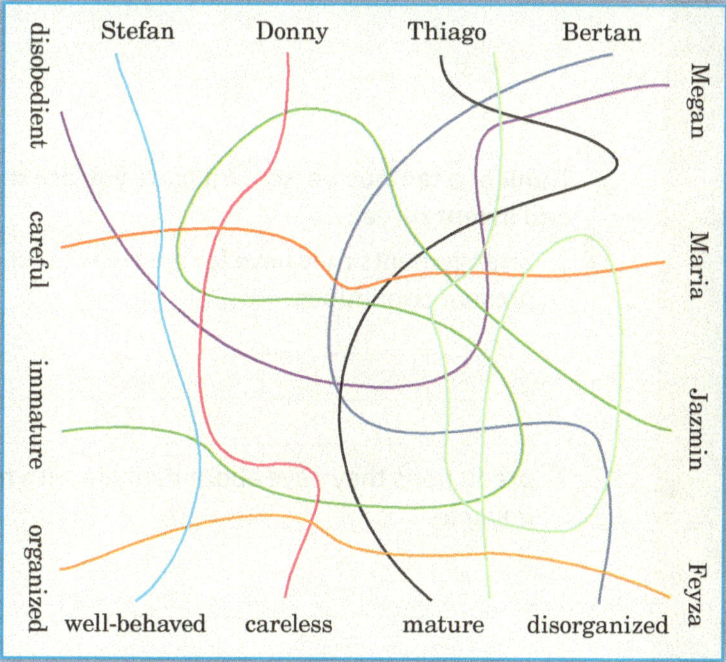

___Stefan: well-behaved; Megan: disobedient___
____
____
____

9 FINISHED?

1 **Find and write seven more travel words. Each word is in a different color.**

a	b		a			t		i	m	
i			j	a	r	k		p	u	k
p		t	d				a		g	
	c		a	n		b		d		o
g		a	n		s		g		o	
	o		o	t	t	e	i		m	k
n		e	i		i			n	i	
	c		e	y		o			o	i
a		c				r		t	n	
r		h		s			c		o	b
	e		d			o		s	n	

1 purple accommodation
2 blue ______
3 dark blue ______
4 red ______
5 orange ______
6 light blue ______
7 yellow ______
8 green ______

2 **Think of a famous person. Imagine you are them and invent three …**

1 arrangements they have for next week with the present continuous.

______
______
______

2 predictions they have about their life with *to be going to*.

______
______
______

3 predictions about next year with the future continuous.

______
______
______

3 **Find five more relative pronouns in the wordsnake. Then complete the sentences with relative clauses so they are true for you.**

tewhosonthatrewhewnhidhatywherenimwhywimwhosewhswhenidal

1 I enjoy things ______
______.
2 I like people ______
______.
3 I don't like things ______
______.
4 I like watching movies ______
______.
5 I often go to places ______
______.
6 I want to know ______
______.

4 **Write the letters in the correct order to make phrasal verbs to complete sentences 1–5. Then write the blue letters in the correct order to make a phrasal verb to complete sentence 6.**

1 We check in to the hotel at 6:30 a.m. (chkienc)
2 What time does the plane ______? (kfatofe)
3 It's was a beautiful city, but we didn't have much time to ______. (laokrnoudo)
4 When you ______ from your vacation, let's have dinner. (cgeaktb)
5 What time should we ______ tomorrow to get to the station? (tfosfe)
6 When does their flight ______?

5 VOCABULARY BANK

Planet Earth

carbon dioxide	energy	pollution	the planet
climate change	marine life	solar power	waste
endangered species	oxygen	the environment	wildlife

1 Match the clues with the words.

1 [ ] We sometimes call Earth this.
2 [ ] Pandas, tigers, elephants, etc.
3 [ ] This is 21 percent of the air we breathe.
4 [ ] We use the sun to make this.
5 [ ] Fish, dolphins, whales, etc.

a marine life
b solar power
c oxygen
d the planet
e endangered species

Natural Environments

bay

cave

cliff

coast

iceberg

rainforest

stream

valley

volcano

waterfall

2 Complete the puzzle to find the mystery word.

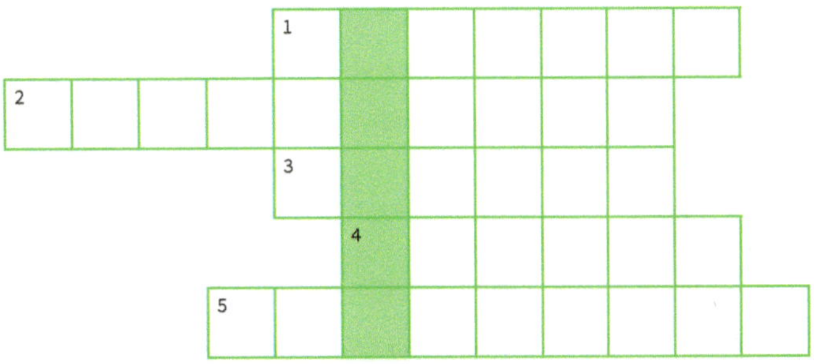

1 a large piece of ice that floats in the sea
2 a hot, wet area with lots of trees
3 a low area between hills or mountains
4 this is smaller than a river
5 water that drops from a high part of a river to a low part

Mystery word ________________

LEARN TO LEARN

Look, Cover, Remember

Use the look, cover, remember technique to help you learn new vocabulary.

3 Look at the pictures above of natural environments for one minute. Then close your book. Write the words you remember. Compare with a partner.

6 VOCABULARY BANK

Making Things

add	pour
boil	press
cover	pull
dip	reduce
freeze	remove
increase	stir
place	

1 **Are the sentences *T* (true) or *F* (false)?**

1 You usually use a knife to stir things. ___
2 You can cook potatoes by boiling them. ___
3 When you reduce a temperature, you make it higher. ___
4 People often cover food to keep insects off it. ___
5 If you remove something, you add it to something. ___

Materials and Containers

cardboard

glass

leather

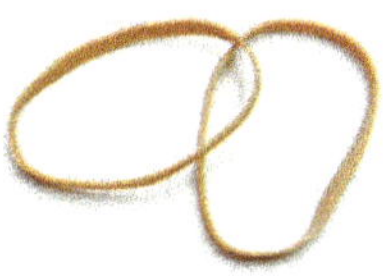
rubber

silk

tin

bag

box

can

case

jar

tube

2 **Circle the correct words to complete the sentences.**

1 Remove the printer from its *leather* / *cardboard* / *rubber* box.
2 We should reduce the number of plastic *bags* / *tubes* / *cans* we use.
3 The scarf was made of *tin* / *leather* / *silk*.
4 When the jam is cool, pour it into the *box* / *bag* / *jar*.
5 When you finish your drawing, place the pencils back in their *can* / *case* / *tube*.

LEARN TO LEARN

Visualizing

Thinking of an image to go with new words can help you remember their meaning.

3 **Write two things from the box that you could use to visualize each word (1–4). Write one more thing for each word. Tell your partner your ideas.**

belt	dress	honey	lemonade	olives	shirt	shoes	soup

1 can ______ ______ ______
2 silk ______ ______ ______
3 jar ______ ______ ______
4 leather ______ ______ ______

7 VOCABULARY BANK

Festivals

atmosphere

ceremony

costume

crowd

decoration

fireworks

fair

float

lantern

parade

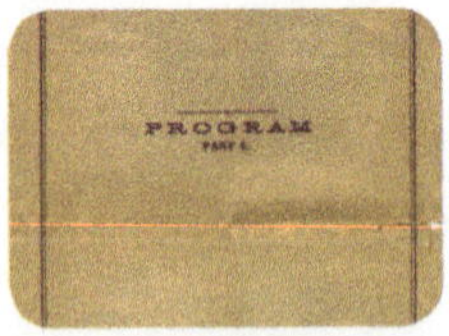

program

stall

1 Complete the sentences with the correct form of the festivals words.

1 The dancers were all wearing amazing ________________.
2 There were several ________________ selling different types of food.
3 We watched the musicians and dancers driving by on a ________________.
4 Everyone was clapping and singing – the ________________ in the hall was great!
5 We checked our ________________ to see what time the band was on.

Music Festivals and Live Music

band member	encore	headliner	supporting act	track
campsite	gig	stage	tent	venue

2 Edwin has been to a festival. What is he talking about? Write the correct music festivals and live music words.

1 "It's a huge field with a stage at one end." ____________
2 "They played for two hours before the main band came on." ____________
3 "In my opinion, it's the best song on their album." ____________
4 "They have a fantastic new guitar player." ____________
5 "It was crowded and the tents were very close together." ____________

LEARN TO LEARN

Stress Patterns

Knowing the stress pattern of a word can help you pronounce it and hear it when people say it.

3 Write the stress pattern for the words 2–6.

1 band member (O o o)
2 campsite
3 encore
4 headliner
5 supporting act
6 venue

8 VOCABULARY BANK

School

cheat on a test

fail an exam

get detention

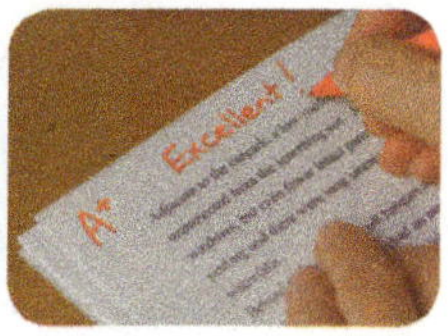

get good grades

give somebody a talk

hand in homework

pass an exam

pay attention to the teacher

study for a test

take an exam

write an essay

1 Match sentences 1–5 with sentences a–e.

1 ☐ She learned some more vocabulary for the topic the evening before.
2 ☐ She listened carefully in class.
3 ☐ Her teacher was angry with her because she was very late for the exam.
4 ☐ She gave her essay to the teacher.
5 ☐ Her grades were good enough to get into college.

a She handed in her homework.
b She passed her exams.
c Her teacher gave her a talk.
d She paid attention to the teacher.
e She studied for a test.

Attitude and Behaviour

careful	disobedient	immature	organized	rude
careless	disorganized	mature	polite	well-behaved

2 Complete the sentences with the words in the box.

careful careless disobedient mature well-behaved

1 You won't pass your exam if you make ________________ mistakes.
2 The teacher gave them a talk because they were ________________ in class.
3 These are difficult words – be ________________ when you spell them.
4 Philip never gets detention because he is so ________________.
5 Elif's attitude toward her school work is very ________________.

LEARN TO LEARN

Personalizing Vocabulary

Using new words to talk about your life helps you remember them.

3 Look at the attitude and behavior words. Which adjectives are true for you? Choose three and explain why to your partner.

I'm sometimes careless. I make silly mistakes on my homework.

9 VOCABULARY BANK

Travel

abroad

accommodation

backpacking

book

cruise ship

destination

journey

resort

sightseeing

tour

tourist attraction

trip

1 Draw lines to match the three parts of each sentence.

1 When I travel abroad,	I've ever visited is	near the coast.
2 I love going	I usually book	local tour guide.
3 When I arrive at	at a resort	the Grand Canyon.
4 The best tourist attraction	my destination,	I always call my parents.
5 I often stay	sightseeing with a	my accommodations online.

Travel Phrasal Verbs

check in	get back	look around
check out	get in	set off
get away	go away	take off

2 Write the words in the correct order to make sentences.

1 from / do / you / get / when / back / your / trip?

____

2 out / you / check / must / of / your / before / 11 / accommodation

____

3 journey / off / on / their / set / to / the / they / coast

____

4 our / at / gets / in / four / train / o'clock

____

5 looked / we / all / tourist / around / the / attractions

____

LEARN TO LEARN

Remembering New Vocabulary

Using new words in a sentence helps you remember them.

3 Choose four travel phrasal verbs and write sentences. Read them to your partner.

____

____

____

____

We checked in to our accommodation at midnight.

6 TECHNOLOGY

WHEN LIONS ATTACK ... GET CREATIVE!

Technology does amazing things for people, and if we get really creative, it can help wildlife, too. That's what Richard Turere discovered after lions attacked his family's **cattle**.

Every year, thousands of cattle in Kenya are killed by lions. This can cost farmers a lot of money, and sometimes they kill the lions to stop the attacks. The situation was serious, until 11-year-old Richard Turere found a clever solution.

He knew the lions never attacked when people were walking around with **flashlights**. This gave him an idea. First, he collected some old flashlights, pulled out the LED lights, and used a long electrical wire to connect them together. Next, he connected an **indicator** box from a motorcycle. This made the lights turn on and off at different times. He put the lights on a fence around the cows. Then he connected an old car battery for power and charged it with a solar panel. When the lights were turned on at night, it looked like someone was moving around with a flashlight.

The lions stopped attacking, so Turere helped set up "lion lights" for many of his neighbors. Lion attacks have dropped 96 percent on farms with the lights.

Sometimes, problems can be solved using a bit of imagination and a few old parts!

1 **Look at the title and the pictures. What do you think the text is about?**

2 **Read the text. Check your answer from Exercise 1.** 6.14

3 **Are the sentences *T* (true) or *F* (false)?**

1. In Kenya, lions kill thousands of cattle each summer. F
2. Richard had his clever idea when he was a teenager. ___
3. Farms that use the lights have no lion attacks. ___
4. Richard's invention makes the lions think people are present. ___

4 **Put the stages to build lion lights in order.**

a ☐ Connect the wire to a battery.
b ☐ Connect lights to an electrical wire.
c ☐ Turn on the lion lights.
d ☐ Charge the battery with a solar panel.
e ☐ Connect the wire to an indicator box.

5 **Complete the sentences with the words in bold in the text.**

1. We use ________ to see when it's dark.
2. ________ are often used for milk and meat.
3. Drivers use an ________ when they turn.

Explore It!

Guess the correct answer.

What do farmers in Kenya put on their fences to stop elephants from eating their plants?

a chemicals b bees c electricity

Find an interesting fact about another invention. Then write a question for your partner to answer.

8 CITIZENSHIP

1 **Discuss the questions.**

1 What is a good citizen?

2 What should students learn at school?

8.11 2 **Read the article. Check your answer to question 1 from Exercise 1.**

3 **Circle the correct answer.**

1 Traditional schools use homework and tests to help students be …

a positive. c good.
b creative. d responsible.

2 Montessori schools allow students to …

a decide what to study.
b leave the classroom.
c teach other students.
d make the rules.

3 Students at the Green School help grow an organic garden to develop …

a creativity. c communication.
b respect for nature. d independence.

4 **Match the words in bold with the definitions.**

1 something that is burned to provide heat or power ______

2 able to work without being told what to do ______

3 parts of a situation or problem ______

Explore It!

Guess the correct answer.

One of these people is not a Montessori graduate. Who is it?

a Prince Harry b Jeff Bezos c Kristen Stewart

Find another interesting fact about education. Then write a question for your partner to answer.

GROWING UP AND GIVING BACK

We all need to help make our communities a better place. That is part of being a good citizen. But how do we learn citizenship?

If you go to a traditional school, your days are probably filled with classes, homework, and tests, which teach you how to be responsible for yourself and for the wider community. They also help you develop communication skills to improve the way you share and understand information, which can have a positive impact on all **aspects** of life and relationships.

Montessori schools use a different approach to help children become independent and useful citizens. Students can choose activities that interest them. This encourages them to be **self-motivated**, to think for themselves, and to be creative. Students attend classes with older and younger students, which inspires them to learn from those around them.

At the Green School in Bali, teachers pay special attention to environmental planning so that students grow up to value and care for our planet. The school has an organic garden and saves **fuel** and energy by using solar and hydro power.

Different schools emphasize different types of citizenship. What is important is that students learn how to respect themselves, each other, and the world around them.

PRONUNCIATION

UNIT 5

Stress in First Conditional Sentences

5.03 **1 Listen and repeat.**

1 If you speak good English, you'll get a better job.
2 I'll go to college if I pass my exams.

2 Underline the stressed words.

1 If he doesn't call, I'll send him a message.
2 You'll meet my friends if you get there early.
3 We'll arrive on time if we leave now.
4 She'll help if we have a problem.

5.04 **3 Listen, check, and repeat.**

UNIT 6

/ɪ/ and /iː/

6.03 **1 Listen and repeat.**

1 /ɪ/ sk**i**n c**i**ty 2 /iː/ coff**ee** r**ea**ch

6.04 **2 Listen and circle the option you hear.**

1 *it / eat*
2 *hit / heat*
3 *live / leave*
4 *ship / sheep*

3 Write the words in the correct place according to the pronunciation of the letters in bold.

~~extr**e**me~~ fr**ee** fr**ee**ze g**i**ve l**i**sten s**i**x sw**i**m t**ea**ch w**ee**k

1 /ɪ/ ______
2 /iː/ extreme, ______

6.05 **4 Listen, check, and repeat.**

5 Take turns saying a word from Exercise 2. Your partner says 1 (/ɪ/) or 2 (/iː/) and repeats the word.

UNIT 7

The Letter *U*

7.03 **1 Listen and repeat.**

1 /ʌ/ l**u**ck 2 /uː/ r**u**le 3 /juː/ **u**niform

2 Write the words in the correct place according to the pronunciation of the letters in bold.

~~f**u**n~~ h**u**ge p**u**nctual r**u**de s**u**bject **u**nit

1 /ʌ/ fun, ______
2 /uː/ ______
3 /juː/ ______

7.04 **3 Listen, check, and repeat.**

4 Write two sentences using words from Exercise 2 in your notebook. Then practice saying them.

UNIT 8

/aɪ/ and /eɪ/

8.02 **1 Listen and repeat.**

1 /aɪ/ n**i**ne fl**y** l**igh**t 2 /eɪ/ l**a**ke d**ay** tr**ai**n

2 Write the words in the correct place according to the pronunciation of the letters in bold.

~~afr**ai**d~~ b**i**te fl**igh**t h**a**te m**ay** m**igh**t pl**ay** r**i**de r**igh**t sh**y** sn**a**ke w**ai**t wh**y**

1 /aɪ/ ______
2 /eɪ/ afraid, ______

8.03 **3 Listen, check, and repeat.**

4 Take turns saying a word from Exercise 2. Your partner writes it in their notebook and repeats it.

UNIT 9

Stress in Compound Nouns

9.02 **1 Listen and repeat.**

1 classroom
2 sunglasses
3 airport
4 solar energy
5 cotton T-shirt
6 glass bottle

2 Underline the stressed word in each compound noun.

1 birthday cake
2 swimming pool
3 airplane tickets
4 plastic chair
5 sunscreen
6 paper plates
7 ice cream
8 sun hat

9.03 **3 Listen, check, and repeat.**

4 Describe a party using the compound nouns from Exercise 2. Use the correct stress.

IRREGULAR VERBS

Infinitive	Simple Past	Past Participle
be	was/were	been
beat	beat	beaten
become	became	become
begin	began	begun
bite	bit	bitten
blow	blew	blown
break	broke	broken
bring	brought	brought
build	built	built
buy	bought	bought
catch	caught	caught
choose	chose	chosen
come	came	come
cost	cost	cost
cut	cut	cut
do	did	done
draw	drew	drawn
drink	drank	drunk
drive	drove	driven
eat	ate	eaten
fall	fell	fallen
feel	felt	felt
fight	fought	fought
find	found	found
fly	flew	flown
forget	forgot	forgotten
get	got	gotten
give	gave	given
go	went	gone
grow	grew	grown
hang	hung	hung
have	had	had
hear	heard	heard
hide	hid	hidden
hit	hit	hit
hold	held	held
hurt	hurt	hurt
keep	kept	kept
know	knew	known
leave	left	left
lend	lent	lent

Infinitive	Simple Past	Past Participle
let	let	let
lie	lied	lied
light	lit	lit
lose	lost	lost
make	made	made
mean	meant	meant
meet	met	met
pay	paid	paid
put	put	put
read	read	read
ride	rode	ridden
ring	rang	rung
rise	rose	risen
run	ran	run
say	said	said
see	saw	seen
sell	sold	sold
send	sent	sent
shine	shone	shone
shoot	shot	shot
show	showed	shown
shut	shut	shut
sing	sang	sung
sit	sat	sat
sleep	slept	slept
speak	spoke	spoken
spend	spent	spent
stand	stood	stood
steal	stole	stolen
swim	swam	swum
take	took	taken
teach	taught	taught
tear	tore	torn
tell	told	told
think	thought	thought
throw	threw	thrown
understand	understood	understood
wake	woke	woken
wear	wore	worn
win	won	won
write	wrote	written

SHAPE IT! 3

COMBO B

WORKBOOK

Annie Cornford and Andrew Reid

CAMBRIDGE
UNIVERSITY PRESS

CONTENTS

5 How can we save our planet?

VOCABULARY

Planet Earth

1 ★ Complete the crossword. Use the clues.

DOWN ↓

1 We usually separate our paper, plastic, and food … into different trash cans.

2 I try to save … at home – I always turn off the lights when I'm not using them.

3 Cycling or walking is better for the … than traveling by car.

5 Governments want to reduce the carbon … (or CO_2) that their countries produce.

8 We all live on … Earth.

ACROSS →

4 Tigers are an … species. It's possible they will all die in a few years.

6 There used to be a lot of … near here, like birds and butterflies, but not now.

7 Trees produce … for us to breathe.

8 Traffic causes a lot of air … in cities.

9 … change causes hotter weather around the world.

10 … power from the sun produces a lot of electricity.

11 Plastic in the ocean is bad for all … life, from large whales to small fish.

Explore It!

Guess the correct answer.

How much of the plastic that we use every year ends up in the seas and oceans?

a 1 percent b 5 percent c 10 percent

Find another interesting fact about pollution in the ocean. Write a question and send it to a classmate in an email, or ask them in the next class.

2 ★★ Complete the notes with words from Exercise 1.

Things We Should Reduce

- *the amount of carbon* [1] dioxide *that we produce*
- [2] ____________ *(e.g., air, water, and noise)*
- [3] ____________ *(e.g., plastic and food)*
- *the effects of* [4] ____________ *change (e.g., rising temperatures and sea levels)*
- *the amount of* [5] ____________ *that we use (e.g., electricity and gas)*

Things We Need to Protect or Save

- *the* [6] ____________ *(the air, our water, etc.)*
- [7] ____________ *life (e.g., fish)*
- [8] ____________ *Earth (our home – we only have one!)*
- *all animals, but especially* [9] ____________ *species (e.g., tigers and gorillas)*

3 ★★★ Circle the correct words.

We face many environmental problems, such as rising levels of [1]*(carbon)* / *oxygen* dioxide in the air, which cause [2]*climate* / *planet* change. Plastic is also a big cause of [3]*pollution* / *energy*. Every year, we put a lot of plastic [4]*energy* / *waste* into our oceans. This is a huge problem for [5]*endangered* / *marine* life. It ends up in the stomachs of fish, which bigger animals then eat, including us. Many animals are therefore becoming [6]*endangered* / *marine*. But plastic is all over the [7]*planet* / *environment*. Even high mountains now have millions of tiny pieces of plastic on them, carried there by the wind.

READING

A News Story

1 ★ Look at the photos and read the news story quickly. Circle the best title.

a Why We Should Use Drinking Straws
b The History of Drinking Straws
c The End of Drinking Straws?

News | Search
Home | News | Articles | Sign In | Register

Most of us have used straws. They are useful and [1] *c* . When we get a soda or juice from a café or restaurant, for example, it often comes with a straw, [2] ______. We usually use them once and then **dispose of** them immediately. In fact, people in the U.S.A. use 500 million every day. That's enough straws to go around the planet 2.5 times!

The big problem with straws is that many of them [3] ______. Europeans **recycle** only about 30 percent of their plastic, and straws are in the top ten **items** of **litter** found on beaches every year.

The good news is that [4] ______. More and more big companies are deciding not to use straws, or to provide them only when customers have asked for them. The city of Seattle, in the U.S.A., has already put a **ban** on straws, and the European Union wants to do the same by 2030. England plans to do this in 2020. Even the British Queen [5] ______.

So, it is possible that plastic drinking straws will soon be a thing of the past. Many people believe that we can continue to protect our environment by also reducing all the other plastic objects that we only use once, [6] ______.

2 ★★ Complete the article with the missing sentence parts (a–f).

a end up in the ocean, as waste
b such as bags, cups, and bottles
~~c they can be fun to drink with~~
d people are starting to do something about the problem
e including when we haven't asked for one
f has decided not to have plastic straws in any of her houses

3 ★★ Match the words in bold in the news story with the definitions.

1 things on a list *items*
2 put something in the trash can after we have used it ______
3 an official law that stops something from happening ______
4 use something again, or change it into something different ______
5 small pieces of trash in public places ______

4 ★★ What do these numbers in the news story describe?

1 30 *percent is the amount of plastic that Europeans recycle*
2 500 million ______
3 2.5 ______
4 2020 ______
5 10 ______

5 ★★★ Apart from a ban, how can we reduce the number of plastic straws people use? Write three ideas.

______
______
______

GRAMMAR IN ACTION

The First Conditional

1 ☆ **Circle the correct options.**

1 If I (see) / *don't* see any litter on the beach, I'll pick it up.
2 I won't use my bike tomorrow *unless* / *if* it's raining. I don't want to get wet.
3 Unless we *use* / *don't use* alternative forms of energy, we will create more air pollution.
4 If you *will leave* / *leave* your computer on all night, it will waste energy.
5 Some cities *may* / *may be* underwater if sea levels rise.
6 I'll travel by train if I *go* / *might go* on vacation this year.

2 ☆☆ **Complete the sentences with the phrases in the box.**

climate change will get worse if we stop using so much plastic ~~it will help the planet~~ many types of plants may be in danger there might be more plastic than fish by 2050 unless we protect them

1 If we reduce our energy use, *it will help the planet*.
2 Many animals could become endangered ______.
3 If we lose a lot of insect species, ______.
4 If we don't reduce the amount of carbon dioxide, ______.
5 Unless we stop polluting our oceans, ______.
6 It will help the planet ______.

3 ☆☆ **Complete the text with the verbs in the box.**

act continue is might be ~~might not see~~ will need

If you drive somewhere on a summer night and check the front window of your car after, you [1] *might not see* many dead insects on it. This doesn't sound like a problem. In fact, if your car [2] ______ clean, you will probably be pleased. However, this is a worrying sign. Over the last 30 years, the number of insects has fallen by 75 percent. But if there are fewer flies and mosquitoes in the future, the world [3] ______ a better place, right? Wrong! The problem is that if insects [4] ______ to disappear, we will all be in trouble. Many plants depend on them. As insects move from one plant to another, they carry pollen, which helps plants grow again. And if the number of people on the planet keeps on rising, we [5] ______ more and more food. Unless we [6] ______ quickly, insect numbers could fall even more. This could be very bad news for both humans and the planet.

4 ☆☆☆ **Complete the second sentence so that it has a similar meaning to the first. Use the word in parentheses.**

1 If we don't do something soon, it's possible that endangered species will disappear.
Endangered species could disappear if we don't do something soon. (could)
2 There will be huge problems if we don't protect our environment.
______ our environment, there will be huge problems. (unless)
3 If we don't stop using chemicals on farms, it's possible that insect numbers will fall.
______ if we don't stop using chemicals on farms. (might)
4 If we do something now, we might stop climate change.
Unless we do something now, we ______ climate change. (might)

5 ☆☆☆ **Complete the sentences with your own ideas.**

1 Unless we do something about climate change, ______.
2 We might be able to help the planet if ______.

VOCABULARY AND LISTENING

Natural Environments

1 ☆ **Look at the photos and complete the natural environment words.**

1 bay

2 v______

3 c______

4 c______

5 c______

6 i______

7 r______

8 s______

9 v______

10 w______

2 ☆ **Choose the three most difficult words to remember in Exercise 1. Then draw a picture of each one in your notebook (see the *Learn to Learn* tip in the Student's Book, p62).**

3 ☆☆ **Circle the correct options.**

1 A *stream* / *bay* is a small river, usually in the country.
2 You only find *icebergs* / *cliffs* in very cold places like the Arctic.
3 A *valley* / *cave* is a big hole in a mountain or under the ground.
4 A *cliff* / *valley* is a high area of vertical rock, often near the ocean.
5 A *stream* / *waterfall* is where a river falls from a high point to a lower point.
6 A *volcano* / *bay* is a mountain with a hole at the top. Sometimes gases and hot liquids come out.
7 A *rainforest* / *waterfall* is a hot place with trees and a lot of animals.
8 A *bay* / *valley* is an area between hills or mountains. There is often a river at the bottom.

A Class Discussion

5.01 **4** ☆ **Listen to the class discussion. Which four natural environments in Exercise 1 do the students mention?**

1 ______ 2 ______
3 ______ 4 ______

5.01 **5** ☆☆ **Listen again and complete the notes.**

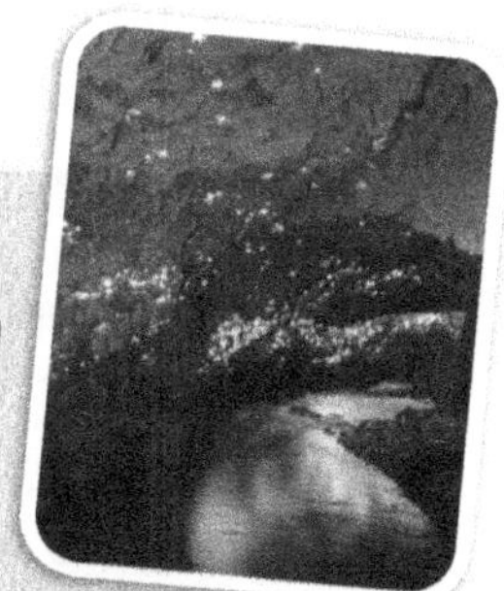

Harry talks about caves in [1] New Zealand. Inside the caves there is a small [2] ______. To travel through the caves, you need to take a [3] ______. If you look up at the top of the cave, you can see thousands of [4] ______ – they look like stars.

Abbie talks about [5] ______ in Papua New Guinea – these are very difficult to get to. There are also rainforests where scientists have found a lot of [6] ______. They have discovered a colorful fish, a river [7] ______, and a tree kangaroo. There are only [8] ______ tenkile tree kangaroos alive today.

6 ☆☆☆ **Think of three examples of natural environments in Exercise 1 that are in your country. What are their names?**

______
______
______

GRAMMAR IN ACTION
The Second Conditional

1 ☆ **Circle the correct options.**

1 If I could travel anywhere in the world, …
  a I'll visit a jungle.
  (b) I'd visit a jungle.
  c I visited a jungle.

2 I don't know what would happen …
  a if all the insects will disappear.
  b if all the insects would disappear.
  c if all the insects disappeared.

3 What would happen if …
  a we cut down all the rainforests?
  b we'd cut down all the rainforests?
  c would we cut down all the rainforests?

4 If I were you, …
  a I'd find out more information.
  b I found out more information.
  c I'm finding out more information.

5 People wouldn't buy plastic products …
  a if they have a better alternative.
  b if they had a better alternative.
  c if they'd have a better alternative.

2 ☆☆ **Complete the second conditional sentences using the verbs in parentheses.**

1 If I _had_ a bike, I _would use_ it to go to school. (have / use)

2 I ________ out today if it ________ cold. (go / not be)

3 If they ________ near the ocean, they ________ to the beach a lot. (live / go)

4 The waterfall ________ more interesting to look at if it ________ raining. (be / be)

5 If we ________ so much meat, we ________ so many rainforests. (not eat / not cut down)

3 ☆☆ **Complete the blog post with the correct form of the verbs in the box to make second conditional sentences.**

be (x3)	~~can~~	check	find	not continue	not use	~~try~~

HOME | ABOUT ME | ARCHIVE | FOLLOW

If I [1] _could_ do anything to help the planet, I [2] _would try_ to stop people from buying so many things with palm oil in them. If you [3] ________ the ingredients in the things you buy, you [4] ________ palm oil in many of them – from cookies to toothpaste. It's a cheap type of oil, and our products [5] ________ more expensive if companies [6] ________ it.

The oil comes from trees that only grow in hot countries. This means that we need to cut down rainforests to grow them. This is a problem for the animals that live in rainforests, including the orangutan. If we [7] ________ to destroy their natural habitat, orangutans wouldn't be endangered. So, if there [8] ________ one useful thing everyone could do to protect the environment, it [9] ________ to buy things that don't contain palm oil.

4 ☆☆ **Write second conditional questions and then write short answers (affirmative or negative).**

1 be so much waste / people not use so much plastic / ? (✗)
  Would _there be so much waste if people didn't use so much plastic?_
  No, there wouldn't.

2 we recycle more waste / help the environment / ? (✓)
  If ________
  ____

3 they use solar power / they have enough sunlight / ? (✓)
  Could ________
  ____

4 companies use palm oil / it not be cheap / ? (✗)
  Would ________
  ____

WRITING

An Opinion Essay

1 ★ **Read the essay. Which environmental problem in the photos (a–c) does the writer think is the most serious?** ______

2 ★★ **Complete the essay with the words in the box. Sometimes more than one answer is possible.**

addition	~~believe~~	Furthermore	
However	opinion	summary	view

Our Most Serious Environmental Problem

There are many environmental problems nowadays, and it is difficult to know which one is the most important. Some people [1] *believe* that we should protect the rainforests. Other people might think that we need to stop using plastic. Which is the most important?

It would be good if we could solve both of these problems. [2] ______, in my [3] ______, the most serious problem is air pollution. This is something that is getting worse in cities around the world. [4] ______, it has an effect on everyone as it is a major cause of health problems, especially in children.

In my [5] ______, the first step would be to reduce the number of cars in cities. This is one of the biggest causes of pollution. In [6] ______, we need to make more people use public transportation or cleaner forms of personal transportation like bicycles. We also need cleaner factories that don't produce dangerous gases that are bad for our health.

In [7] ______, if we have cleaner cities with cleaner air, we will all become healthier. We will also spend more time outdoors, exercising and enjoying our natural environment.

3 ★★ **Circle the correct options.**

1 The first paragraph includes an introduction and *a question / the writer's main opinion*.

2 The second paragraph gives *the writer's main / other people's* opinion.

3 The third paragraph offers *reasons for / possible solutions to* the problem.

4 The last paragraph *introduces / summarizes* the writer's opinion.

PLAN

4 ★★ **Write your own opinion essay. Decide what you think is the biggest environmental problem and think of two possible solutions to the problem. Take notes.**

Problem: ______

Solution 1: ______

Solution 2: ______

5 **Decide what information to include in each paragraph. Use the information in Exercise 3 to help you.**

WRITE

6 ★★★ **Write your opinion essay. Remember to include four paragraphs, the first and second conditional, and words and phrases from the *Useful Language* box (see Student's Book, p65).**

CHECK

7 **Do you …**

- have an introduction with a question for the reader to think about?
- have solutions and examples to support your opinion?
- have a conclusion?

5 REVIEW

VOCABULARY

1 Match the beginnings of the sentences (1–10) with the ends (a–j).

1 Too much carbon ☐
2 It's important to save ☐
3 The biggest environmental problem is climate ☐
4 We all need to recycle and reduce waste to help protect the ☐
5 Plastic is a big problem for marine ☐
6 Plants produce ☐
7 The white rhino is ☐
8 We all live on the same ☐
9 Cars are the main cause of air ☐
10 Sunny countries produce a lot of energy from ☐

a change.
b an endangered species.
c oxygen, which all animals need to survive.
d planet, so we should take care of it.
e life, like fish, whales, and sea birds.
f dioxide causes global warming.
g pollution in cities.
h energy and not waste it.
i solar power.
j environment.

2 Match the sentences with the words in the box.

cave cliff coast icebergs rainforest stream volcano waterfall

1 We walk here by the water as it flows through the forest. ______
2 My grandparents have a house there. It's nice because you can just walk out onto the beach and you can hear the ocean at night. ______
3 You can walk into it and it's really interesting. It's dark, but you can hear the sound of water deep below you. ______
4 Don't stand too close to the edge. I know it's nice to look down at the ocean, but it can be dangerous. ______
5 They cut down a large area. It will take hundreds of years for the trees and plants to grow again. ______
6 They're very dangerous to boats and ships. Remember that you can only see 10 percent of them. The rest is below the ocean. ______
7 Every second, almost 3 million liters of water drops to the river below at Niagara! ______
8 It's still active and you can often smell the gases – the heat and noise is incredible sometimes! ______

GRAMMAR IN ACTION

3 Mark (✓) the correct sentences and correct five incorrect sentences.

1 If I pass my exam tomorrow, I am really happy. ☐
______
2 I might go for a drive along the coast tomorrow if the weather will be nice. ☐
______
3 Will you call me if you're late? ☐
______
4 Unless I don't do my homework now, I won't have time to go out later. ☐
______
5 If I will have money, I will go to the movies on Friday. ☐
______
6 I won't buy a new phone unless this one breaks completely. ☐
______
7 If you look in the stream, you will may see some fish. ☐
______
8 You could take a break if you feel tired. ☐
______

4 Complete the sentences with the words in the box.

didn't have | had | knew | took | was | were | would be | would have | would need | would stop | would take | wouldn't be

1 If I __________ time, I __________ a trip to the bay.
2 The town __________ in trouble if that volcano __________ active.
3 If you __________ more sociable, you __________ more friends.
4 You __________ sick if you __________ better care of yourself.
5 If I __________ a bike, I __________ to use the bus.
6 More people __________ eating meat if they __________ about the effects on the environment.

CUMULATIVE GRAMMAR

5 Complete the text with the missing words. Circle the correct options.

I [1] ______ a TV documentary last month about marine life and plastic. Every day, we [2] ______ a lot of plastic waste into the oceans, and even a little drinking straw can have a terrible effect on an animal. For example, if a fish [3] ______ one, it could easily die. And if a sea bird ate the fish, it [4] ______ the plastic, too. Plastic in the oceans is a big problem because it [5] ______ away. It just breaks down into smaller and smaller pieces! [6] ______ we do something about this problem, it will get worse. So, I [7] ______ to make some changes to my life. They're small, but if everyone [8] ______ something small, it would add up to something big. In the past, I [9] ______ a lot of plastic straws and bags. I [10] ______ straws without thinking about it in cafés. Now, I just say I don't need one when they offer. They haven't stopped using straws in cafés in my city [11] ______, but I hope they do soon. Anyway, we all need to do something. If we don't, then soon we [12] ______ to enjoy the natural beauty of the ocean and its marine life.

	a	b	c
1	have watched	watched	watch
2	have put	used to put	put
3	eats	would eat	will eat
4	ate	would eat	will eat
5	doesn't go	wouldn't go	isn't going
6	If	Furthermore	Unless
7	have decided	am deciding	will decide
8	did	does	would do
9	use to use	used to use	did use
10	will use	am using	have used
11	yet	already	since
12	couldn't	can't	won't be able

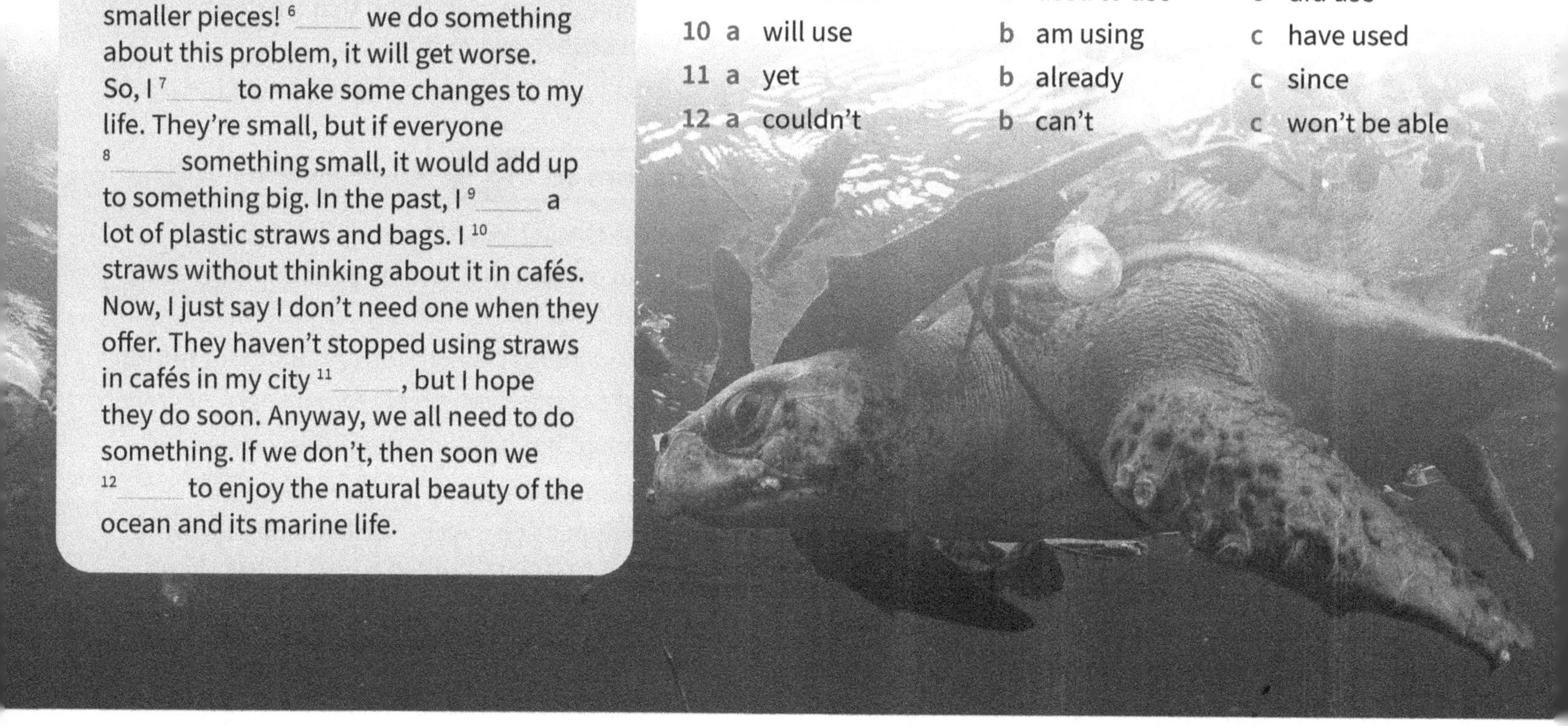

6 How can inventions change our lives?

VOCABULARY

Making Things

1 ☆ **Circle 12 more verbs in the word snake.**

(increase)stirboiladdremovedipplacepullcoverfreezepourreducepress

2 ☆☆ **Complete the sentences with the correct form of the verbs in Exercise 1.**

1 *Increase* the oven temperature from 150°C to 200°C.
2 I want to ____________ the time I spend watching TV from four hours to one hour a day.
3 Water ____________ at 100°C.
4 She ____________ her feet in the ocean for a few seconds – it was really cold!
5 ____________ the hot water into the cup and ____________ sugar and milk.
6 ____________ the cake from the oven and ____________ it on a plate to cool.
7 You should ____________ the soup with a spoon so it doesn't burn and stick to the pot.
8 I ____________ my eyes so I couldn't see the frightening scenes in the movie.
9 Lara collects flowers – she ____________ them flat and puts them in a scrapbook.
10 We use our car to ____________ our camper when we go on vacation.
11 You should ____________ fresh fish at –20°C for at least seven days before eating it.

3 ☆ **Choose one of the words in Exercise 1 and think of an image to go with it. Draw your image in your notebook (see the *Learn to Learn* tip in the Student's Book, p71).**

4 ☆☆ **Circle the correct words.**

1 When the milk boils, (*pour*) / *pull* it into your coffee cup.
2 *Reduce* / *Increase* the temperature so that it's really cold.
3 Take a spoon and *remove* / *stir* the butter, sugar, and milk together for a few minutes.
4 *Add* / *Cover* the glass with paper and put it in the fridge overnight.
5 I'll *freeze* / *press* any food that we don't eat, and we can have it next month.
6 Don't *dip* / *freeze* your finger into the hot liquid!

Explore It!

Guess the correct answer.

A chef in the U.S.A. invented chips when he …

a accidentally cooked some potatoes for too long.
b cut potatoes very thinly for an angry customer.
c poured hot fat over some frozen vegetables.

Find another interesting fact about an invention or discovery. Write a question and send it to a classmate in a text, or ask them in the next class.

READING

A News Story

1 ★★ **Read the news story. Complete the paragraphs (1–4) with the headings.**

What Was the Problem? | What Do People Use It for Now? | What Was the Solution? | Who Was Vesta Stoudt?

The Story of Duct Tape

1 ______

In the early 1940s, the U.S. army was fighting in Europe in World War II. Vesta Stoudt was a woman from Illinois who had two sons in the military. As part of the war effort, she was working in a factory in the U.S.A. Her job was to **inspect** and pack equipment for the soldiers in Europe.

2 ______

At the factory, they closed and **secured** the boxes of equipment using a thin paper **tape**. However, the boxes were difficult to open quickly, especially when they were wet. Vesta was worried that soldiers' lives might be in danger because they might not be able to get their equipment out fast enough.

3 ______

Vesta suggested that they close the boxes with a stronger, **waterproof** tape. She designed a basic **prototype** of how she thought the tape should be. The boxes were easier to open quickly with this new tape. Vesta's managers in the factory didn't listen to her, but she didn't give up. She decided to write to Franklin Roosevelt, the president of the United States.

4 ______

The letter worked and Vesta received a letter of thanks from Roosevelt. The government then asked a company to make the tape based on Vesta's idea. The tape was a great success and probably helped save lives! Nowadays, duct tape, as it is known, is used for many different things and in many different industries. It is used by NASA on its spaceships, and clothes are even made from it. And it's all thanks to the **patience** of one inspiring woman.

2 ★★ **Match the words in bold in the news story with the meanings.**

1 made safe from damage *secured*
2 stopping liquid from entering somewhere ______
3 the ability to stay calm and continue doing something difficult ______
4 view closely to check condition ______
5 a long, narrow piece of material we use to close things ______
6 the first example of something ______

3 ★★ **Read the news story again and answer the questions.**

1 Where did Vesta Stoudt work?
She worked in a factory in the U.S.A.
2 What did Vesta do at the factory?
______
3 What problem did Vesta want to solve?
______
4 Why was Vesta's prototype better than the paper tape?
______
5 How did Vesta show patience?
______
6 What examples does the writer give of how people use duct tape now?
______

4 ★★★ **Can you think of any other ways people use duct tape? Write two ideas.**

______

GRAMMAR IN ACTION

Simple Present Passive

1 ★ Complete the chart with the past participle form of the verbs. Mark if the verb is *R* (regular) or *I* (irregular).

Verb	Past Participle	R	I
add	*added*	✓	
break			
catch			
collect			
connect			
design			
develop			
eat			
manufacture			
throw			

2 ★★ Complete the sentences with the simple present passive form of the verbs in parentheses.

1 How many smartphones *are made* every year in Asia? (make)

2 Something new and exciting ________ every day. (invent)

3 The potatoes ________ in very hot oil to make chips. (place)

4 These new inventions ________ enough, in my opinion. (not test)

5 ________ these materials ________ online or should we go to a store? (sell)

3 ★★ Complete the sentences with the simple present passive form of verbs in Exercise 1.

1 Food waste *is collected* for recycling.

2 Sugar ________ to chocolate to make it sweet.

3 How many plastic bottles ________ in the trash every day?

4 New ideas ________ here by brilliant young inventors.

5 ________ your computer ________ to the Internet by a cable or Wi-Fi?

6 This system ________ to help blind people use a computer.

4 ★★ Write questions in the simple present passive. Then write the correct answers using the places in parentheses.

1 coffee beans / grow / Iceland? (South America)

Are coffee beans grown in Iceland?

No, they aren't. Coffee beans are grown in South America.

2 most chocolate / produce / in Switzerland? (the U.S.A.)

____

____

3 these cars / manufacture / in Malta? (China)

____

____

4 insects / eat / in the UK? (Thailand)

____

____

5 bananas / grow / in Denmark? (Ecuador)

____

____

5 ★★★ Complete the text with the simple present passive form of the verbs in parentheses.

It's difficult to believe, but glass [1] *is made* (make) of liquid sand. That's right, the same sand that [2] ________ (find) on the beach or in the desert. When sand [3] ________ (heat) to about 1,700°C, it changes into a liquid. Other minerals[4] ________ (add), and when it cools to a much lower temperature, it changes into glass. To make glass containers, like jars and bottles, liquid glass [5] ________ (pour) into containers in a particular shape, called molds. Of course, glass [6] ________ also ________ (use) for windows, and we [7] ________ (protect) by glass, for example, in cars, but glass breaks easily, too. Glass [8] ________ easily ________ (recycle), so manufacturers can often use the same glass again and again in their products.

VOCABULARY AND LISTENING

Materials and Containers

1 ☆ **Match the materials with the containers in the box to make six objects. Then write the words in the correct column. Use each word only once.**

~~bag~~ box can cardboard case glass jar leather rubber ~~silk~~ tin tube

Material	Container
[1] silk	bag
2	
3	
4	
5	
6	

2 ☆☆ **Complete the sentences with the objects in Exercise 1.**

1 Julia's dress doesn't have pockets. She needs a little silk bag to put her phone and wallet in.
2 A garden hose is a ______________. It's long and thin. You use it to water your flowers.
3 When Dad goes to work every morning, he carries his laptop and all his important papers in a ______________.
4 Our new computer came in a big ______________. We used it to put old books and clothes in.
5 Tuna, peas, and beans – what other things come in a ______________?
6 My grandma used to have a ______________ full of candy and chocolate for visiting children.

A Conversation

3 ☆ **Look at the questions and think about possible answers.**

1 What are jeans made of?
2 Who wears jeans?
3 How much do jeans cost?
4 What are the best styles?
5 What effect do jeans have on the environment?

6.01 **4** ☆ **Listen to two friends shopping for jeans. Which three questions in Exercise 3 do the girls discuss?**

____

6.01 **5** ☆☆ **Listen again. Are the sentences *T* (true) or *F* (false)? Correct the false sentences.**

1 Nicole prefers white jeans to blue jeans. F
Nicole prefers blue jeans.
2 The word "denim" comes from the name of a French town. ___
____
3 Camila says good jeans can cost about $100. ___
____
4 Nicole says that some jeans factories use too much energy. ___
____
5 Nicole says Camila should find out information before she buys jeans. ___
____
6 Camila doesn't want to go to the store that Nicole suggests. ___
____

GRAMMAR IN ACTION

Simple Past Passive

1 Complete the sentences with the simple past passive form of the verbs in parentheses.

1 Tolstoy's novel *War and Peace* was published (publish) in 1867.

2 The world's most expensive violins ____________ (make) by Antonio Stradivari.

3 Facebook ____________ (start) by Harvard University students in 2004.

4 Is it true that some of Shakespeare's plays ____________ (not write) by him?

5 A lot of my photos ____________ (lose) when my phone broke.

6 Paper ____________ (not invent) in Europe but in China.

2 Write questions in the simple past passive.

1 when / first antibiotic / discover?

When was the first antibiotic discovered?

2 where / the world's first subway / open?

____

3 where / the first modern Olympics / hold?

____

4 what / the first Pixar movie / call?

____

5 where / the largest Egyptian pyramids / build?

____

6 when / the first email / write?

____

7 where / the first CD / make?

____

8 when / Google / start?

____

3 Match the answers in the box with the questions in Exercise 2. Check your answers on the Internet if necessary. Then write sentences in the simple past passive.

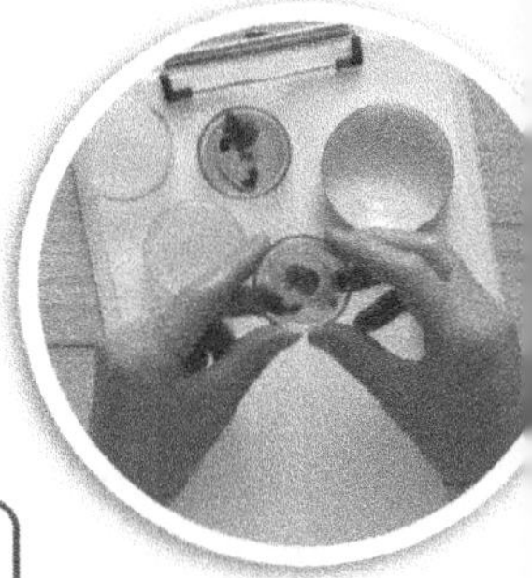

~~1928~~ 1971 1998 Athens Germany Giza London *Toy Story*

1 The first antibiotic was discovered in 1928.

2 ____________

3 ____________

4 ____________

5 ____________

6 ____________

7 ____________

8 ____________

4 Read the text about Stonehenge. Rewrite the underlined phrases using the simple past passive.

Who built Stonehenge and why [1]someone built it continues to be a great mystery. It is one of the most famous prehistoric monuments in the UK. [2]Someone started the building of Stonehenge about 5,000 years ago. Some people believe that [3]someone used Stonehenge in a celebration of the sun. [4]Someone designed it in exact mathematical detail, as the stone circle perfectly matches the direction of the midsummer sunrise and the midwinter sunset. There are two types of stone at Stonehenge. The larger stones are called "sarsens." The tallest sarsen stands nine meters high and weighs 25 tons – [5]someone carried the stones 32 kilometers to Stonehenge! The smaller "bluestones" weigh much less, but [6]someone brought these stones from Wales, a distance of 225 kilometers. Nobody knows how [7]someone transported such heavy stones so far in those days.

1 it was built

2 ____________

3 ____________

4 ____________

5 ____________

6 ____________

7 ____________

WRITING

A Review

1 ☆ **Look at the photo and read the review. Is everything about the smartwatch positive?**

____

1 If you're serious about your fitness training, you'll find this smartwatch very helpful. It counts the calories used in every activity you do. It also gives information on goals, such as distance and speed, and tells you your heart rate. You can connect it to your favorite fitness apps so that your performance can help improve your training.

2 This smartwatch is light and comfortable. The strap looks like silk, though it's actually made from soft rubber. It looks cool and modern, and it feels like silk on your skin, too, so you won't know you're wearing it! It's also waterproof, so you can walk straight into the shower after your workout. The battery life is very good: it lasts up to 20 hours and it recharges very quickly.

3 What I like about this smartwatch is that it's sporty and strong, but it's also really comfortable, so you can wear it all day. However, I should point out that it's not cheap. Overall, I think it's a really cool invention and I'm really happy I bought this model!

2 ☆☆ **Read the review again. In which paragraph (1–3) can you find …**

a a description of what the invention does? [1]
b what the reviewer likes the most? [ ]
c a physical description? [ ]
d the reviewer's general opinion? [ ]
e a disadvantage? [ ]
f who the invention is for? [ ]

3 ☆☆ **Put the words in the correct order to make the *Useful Language* phrases.**

1 made from / soft rubber / is / The strap
The strap is made from soft rubber.

2 it's a / really cool invention / Overall, / I think
____

3 it's sporty and strong / about this smartwatch / is that / What I like
____

4 it's not cheap / point out that / I should / However,
____

5 The strap / looks / silk / like
____

PLAN

4 ☆☆ **Write your own review. Choose an amazing digital device or gadget and take notes.**

Who the device or gadget is for: ______________________________

What it does: ______________________________

What it looks like: ______________________________

The advantages: ______________________________

One disadvantage: ______________________________

Your opinion: ______________________________

WRITE

5 ☆☆☆ **Write your review. Remember to include the parts of the review from Exercise 2, the passive, and phrases from the *Useful Language* box (see Student's Book, p77).**

CHECK

6 **Do you …**

- describe what the device/gadget does and who it's for?
- give a physical description?
- say what the advantages/disadvantages are?
- give your general opinion?

6 REVIEW

VOCABULARY

1 Match the beginnings of the sentences (1–8) with the ends (a–h).

1 If the fruit has pits in it, ☐
2 You should reduce the ☐
3 Don't dip your fingers into ☐
4 Palm oil boils ☐
5 Add the sugar to the water ☐
6 We waited for the liquid to freeze ☐
7 Carefully pour the liquid ☐
8 Pull the paper off the ☐

a temperature when the sauce gets too hot.
b at about 300°C.
c solid before we ate the ice pops.
d and stir both of them together.
e into the molds.
f remove them before you cook it.
g ice pops before the children eat them.
h very hot water – it's dangerous!

2 Underline and correct one mistake with materials and containers in each sentence.

1 The clothes and shoes were packed in cardboard jars. ______
2 It's better to use glass boxes for jam so you can recycle them. ______
3 We gave our mom a pretty silk tube for her birthday. ______
4 We don't know what is in this tin bag because there's no label. ______
5 Our teacher always carries our homework and exam papers in a leather can. ______
6 Hospitals have a lot of rubber cases for medical use. ______

GRAMMAR IN ACTION

3 Complete the conversation with the simple present passive form of the verbs in parentheses.

RYAN Do you know how much coffee [1] ______ (make) every year?
HARI I'm sure it's a lot. I know that loads of coffee [2] ______ (use) in my house!
RYAN Well, they estimate that over two billion cups of coffee [3] ______ (drink) worldwide every day.
HARI Wow! That is amazing! And where [4] ______ all that coffee ______ (grow)? South America?
RYAN Yes, well, most of the coffee that [5] ______ (buy) in the U.S.A. [6] ______ (produce) in Brazil.
HARI I guess the climate is just right there.
RYAN Yes, it's perfect because coffee [7] ______ (plant) in the wet season, but sunshine [8] ______ (need) later in the process. The coffee beans [9] ______ (dry) in the sun and [10] ______ (test) by experts.
HARI Hmm, how about a cup right now?
RYAN Good idea!

4 **Put the words in the correct order to make simple past passive questions. Then write answers using the words in parentheses.**

1 was / When / the / build / Taj Mahal / ? (around 1640)

____

____

2 open / was / this / When / middle school / ? (in 2010)

____

____

3 were / Where / these / make / computers / ? (in Japan)

____

____

4 cave paintings / were / those / Where / old / find / ? (in France)

____

____

5 was / Where / tea / grow / first / ? (in China)

____

____

6 write / was / When / *Macbeth* / ? (in 1606)

____

____

CUMULATIVE GRAMMAR

5 **Complete the text with the missing words. Circle the correct options.**

I [1]______ an interesting article about important inventions the other day. [2]______ that plastic shopping bags [3]______ in the 1960s by a Swedish engineer? Before plastic was invented, shoppers [4]______ paper bags. These were much better for the environment. Nowadays, governments [5]______ to find ways to reduce the use of plastic bags. Ideas include "Bags for Life." These bags [6]______ of cotton and are very strong, so shoppers can use them again and again. Supermarkets have also [7]______ charging customers for their plastic bags. The article also said that scientists believe they [8]______ a special bacteria that [9]______ eat plastic. The bacteria was discovered in a Japanese recycling center in 2016. While the scientists [10]______ the bacteria, they accidentally made it even better at eating plastic! At the moment, the bacteria can only eat the plastic in drink bottles, but in the future, it [11]______ be able to eat all types of plastic! If scientists [12]______ a super bacteria to eat all plastic, plastic bags would become a thing of the past!

	a	b	c
1	read	have read	did read
2	Were you knowing	Did you knew	Did you know
3	was invented	were invented	invented
4	used to use	use to use	use to using
5	try	tried	are trying
6	are made	is made	made
7	begin	begun	began
8	invented	are invented	have invented
9	can	can to	can will
10	investigated	have investigated	were investigating
11	might	can	may not
12	would create	could create	might create

7 What do you celebrate?

1 a *fair* / *parade*

2 *an atmosphere* / *a stall*

VOCABULARY

Festivals

1 ☆ **Look at the photos and circle the correct options.**

2 ☆☆ **Complete the article with the correct form of words in Exercise 1.**

3 a *costume* / *decoration*

4 a *parade* / *float*

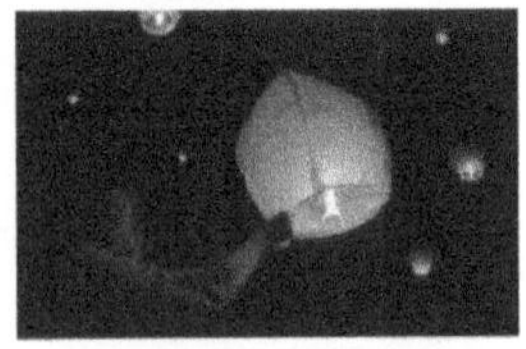

5 a *lantern* / *fireworks*

6 *decorations* / *a float*

7 a *program* / *fair*

8 a *parade* / *program*

9 *fireworks* / *a lantern*

Celebrations Around the World

One of the biggest festivals in Japan is the Gion Festival in Narita, a small town near Tokyo. It's a celebration of the summer. There are colorful [1] *decorations* all over the town, and people dress up in traditional Japanese [2] __________. Visitors can enjoy food and drinks at the many [3] __________ in Narita's narrow streets. The best part of the festival is when decorated [4] __________ with people on them are pulled through the streets to Narita's main temple. The streets of Narita are beautiful at night when they are lit up by [5] __________ on the sides of the buildings.

New Year's Eve is always special in Sydney, Australia. You can see a beautiful display of [6] __________ in the night sky, with thousands exploding over the Sydney Opera House. There are a lot of things to do during the day, too. Children can enjoy fantastic rides at the [7] __________, like a 40-meter Ferris wheel or a super-fast train. In the evening, people love the [8] __________ of boats traveling up and down the harbor with special lights on them!

3 ☆☆ **Circle the correct options.**

1 There was already *a crowd* / *an atmosphere* of 50,000 people at ten o'clock!

2 The band marched in the *ceremony* / *parade* down Main Street.

3 Great music and a lot of people usually make a good *program* / *atmosphere*.

4 A *fair* / *ceremony* is usually a formal event with a long history.

4 ☆☆ **Underline the stressed syllable in each word.**

Two Syllables	Three Syllables	Four Syllables
costume	atmosphere	ceremony
fireworks		decoration
lantern		
parade		

Explore It!

Guess the correct answer.

The famous Japanese … ceremony began around 700 years ago.

a tea b coffee c milk

Find another interesting fact about an ancient ceremony. Write a question and send it to a classmate in an email, or ask them in the next class.

READING

A Folktale

1 **Look at the pictures. What do you think the folktale is about? Read the story and circle the correct answer.**

a a prince who lost his son

b a very brave dog

c a brave prince who killed a wolf

2 **Match the words in bold in the folktale with the meanings.**

1 very shocked horrified

2 a long piece of metal used for fighting ______

3 chasing and trying to catch and kill an animal ______

4 a place in the ground where a dead body is put ______

5 strong and not changing in your friendship with someone ______

6 put something into a hole in the ground and covered it ______

3 **Read the folktale again. Circle the correct answers.**

1 Why did the prince have dogs?

a because he was lonely

b to take care of his castle

c to look for other animals

2 What did the prince think when he saw blood on his dog?

a His son was hurt.

b Something was missing.

c The dog was hurt.

3 What did the dog do?

a He killed the prince's son.

b He killed a dangerous animal.

c He hid behind a bed.

4 What happened at the end?

a Everyone forgot about the dog.

b The village was given the dog's name.

c The prince found another dog.

The Wolf and a Baby Boy

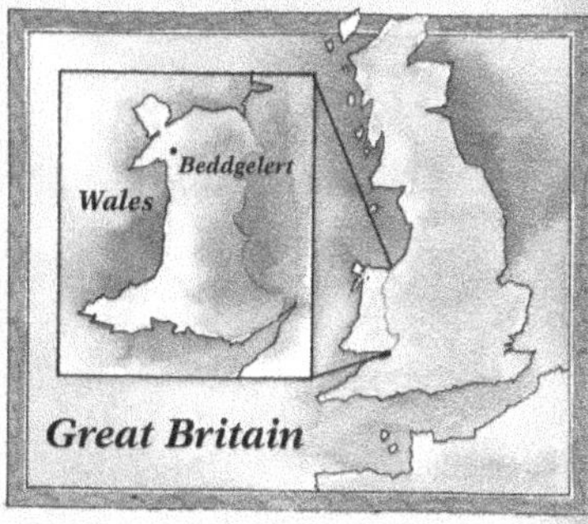

In the north of Wales, there is a small village named Beddgelert. According to an old story, many hundreds of years ago, a prince lived in the area. It was a place of forests and dangerous wild animals. The prince loved **hunting**, so he had many dogs. They spent a lot of time chasing animals through the forests for sport. His favorite dog was named Gelert – a **faithful** dog who the prince loved.

One day, the prince decided to go hunting and called for Gelert. To the prince's surprise, the dog came with blood around its mouth. The prince was **horrified**. Where had the blood come from? He had a terrible thought. He ran to his son's bedroom and saw an awful sight. His baby was missing and the floor was covered in blood. The prince realized what the dog had done. With anger, he took a **sword** and killed Gelert. Seconds later, the prince heard a cry from behind the bed. There was his son, completely safe. And next to his son was a wolf – killed by Gelert, just a few minutes earlier. The prince felt very sad. He carried his favorite dog outside and **buried** it under some stones.

Beddgelert means "Gelert's grave" in the Welsh language, and you can see stones marking the **grave** in the village. However, the story might not be true. Some people say that a hotel owner placed the stones there 200 years ago and, perhaps, invented the story to bring in more tourists. And it worked! Now there are many events in the town, from music festivals to fireworks displays on New Year's Eve. In the summer, people in the town grow lots of flowers as decorations, and Beddgelert has won competitions for being the most beautiful town in the country!

4 **Think of a folktale from your country. Write a paragraph about it in your notebook.**

GRAMMAR IN ACTION

Past Perfect

1 ☆ Match sentences 1–6 with a–f.

1 I felt very tired. [f]
2 I couldn't go to the concert. [ ]
3 I already knew the story of the movie. [ ]
4 I said I was sorry for being late. [ ]
5 I got lost when I went to Quito. [ ]
6 I didn't know what time the concert started. [ ]

a I hadn't looked at the program.
b I hadn't bought any tickets.
c I had read the book.
d I hadn't finished my work on time.
e I hadn't been there before.
f I hadn't slept enough.

2 ☆☆ Read the sentences. (Circle) the action that happened first, *A* or *B*.

1 She went to see the fireworks because her friends had invited her.
A She went to see the fireworks.
(B) Her friends invited her.
2 When I saw the program, I knew I'd seen the show before.
A I saw the program.
B I saw the show.
3 They'd arranged to meet at the food stall, but Tom couldn't find Katy.
A They arranged to meet.
B Tom couldn't find Katy.
4 After he'd called his mom, he ordered a pizza.
A He ordered a pizza.
B He called his mom.
5 Megan felt a little upset after she'd said goodbye to them.
A Megan said goodbye to them.
B She felt a little upset.

3 ☆☆ Complete the sentences with the past perfect form of the verbs in parentheses.

1 I hadn't bought (not buy) a costume, so I didn't have anything special to wear to the parade.
2 Talia __________ (not hear) of the festival before she went there.
3 He got to the concert 20 minutes after it __________ (start).
4 They went to Miami last year, and they were also there 30 years ago. It __________ (change) a lot.
5 We didn't want to see the new *Bond* movie because we __________ (not see) the previous one yet.
6 When I got home, I realized that I __________ (leave) my phone at school.

4 ☆☆ (Circle) the correct options.

PAULA [1](*Did you go*) / *Had you been* anywhere interesting for your vacation?

MARCO Well, I [2]*visited* / *had visited* my grandparents in northern Italy in September. They took me to a town named Marostica. I [3]*didn't go* / *hadn't been* there before.

PAULA Was it nice?

MARCO Yes, they have a chess festival there.

PAULA Chess festival? That doesn't sound very interesting!

MARCO But it was! My grandparents [4]*told* / *had told* me a lot about it before I [5]*went* / *had been*, and I'd thought the same as you. But there was a giant chess set in the middle of the town! And people were dressed in costumes as chess pieces, and they [6]*moved* / *had moved* around the board.

PAULA Oh, do they do that every year?

MARCO Every two years. It's to celebrate a famous chess match that two princes [7]*played* / *had played* about 600 years ago. They [8]*fell* / *had fallen* in love with the same woman, but instead of fighting, they decided to play chess!

VOCABULARY AND LISTENING

Music Festivals and Live Music

1 ☆ **Complete the lists with the words in the box. One word can go in more than one list.**

~~band member~~ campsite encore gig headliner stage supporting act tent track venue

1 where you can see a band: ______________ ______________ ______________

2 where you can stay the night: ______________ ______________

3 singers or musicians: band member ______________ ______________ ______________

4 ways to hear a song ______________ ______________ ______________

2 ☆☆ **Complete the text with the correct form of words in Exercise 1.**

The [1] venue for the Coachella Festival is a polo club in California. Thousands of music fans go there to see their favorite bands. [2] ______________ at Coachella have included some of the biggest names in music, like Radiohead and Beyoncé. There are also lots of interesting, less famous [3] ______________ to see. These bands play on smaller [4] ______________ in front of smaller crowds. Visitors to the festival can stay at a big [5] ______________ with a lot of [6] ______________. There's always a great atmosphere at Coachella, and the bands always leave the fans shouting for an [7] ______________.

A Conversation

7.01 **3** ☆ **Listen to the conversation. What is unusual about the Secret Solstice Festival?**

____

7.01 **4** ☆☆ **Listen again. Are the sentences *T* (true) or *F* (false)?**

1 Antonio hasn't been to the Secret Solstice Festival. T

2 The weather isn't very cold at the festival. ___

3 Famous bands don't play at the festival. ___

4 One of the venues is in a dangerous place. ___

5 Antonio's brother didn't have a ticket for the volcano gig. ___

5 ☆☆ **Look at Exercise 6. What type of information (object, number, or place) is missing in 1–7? (See the *Learn to Learn* tip in the Student's Book, page 86).**

____

7.01 **6** ☆☆☆ **Complete the summary about the Secret Solstice festival. Then listen again and check.**

The Secret Solstice is a festival. It takes place each year in [1] Iceland during the summer solstice. Antonio says the festival feels like a [2] ______________- hour day. When Antonio's brother went, there were about [3] ______________ bands. One venue at the festival was inside a volcano. You needed to fly in a [4] ______________ to get there and then go down [5] ______________ meters to reach the venue. Only [6] ______________ people could see the gig, and the tickets cost about [7] ______________ dollars each.

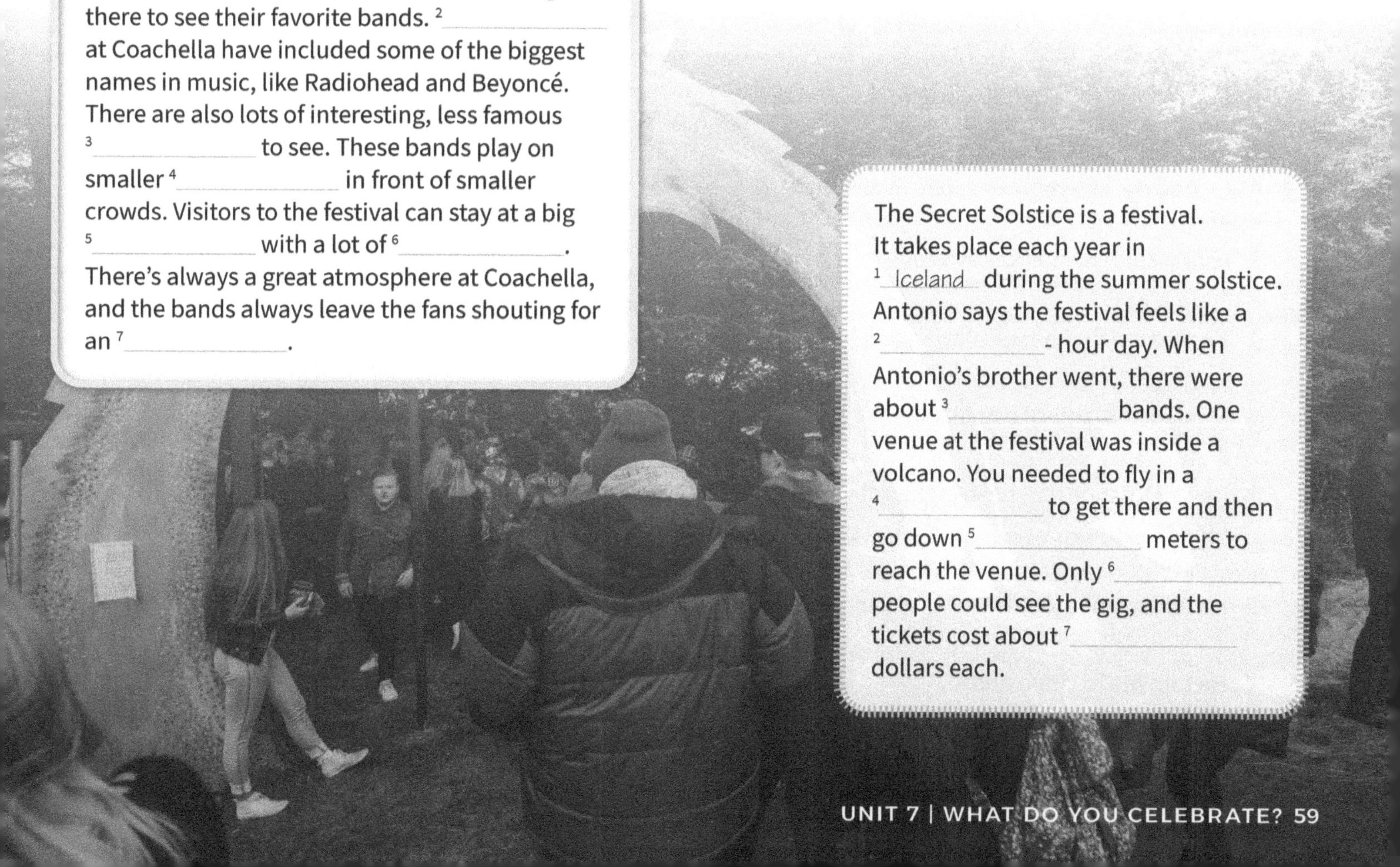

GRAMMAR IN ACTION

Reported Statements

1 ☆ How do the tenses and verbs change in reported speech? Complete the table.

Direct Speech	Reported Speech
Simple Present	1 Simple Past
Simple Past	2
Present Perfect	3
Present Continuous	4
Will	5
Can	6

2 ☆ Complete the sentences with *said* or *told*.

1 My sister __said__ she went to a really interesting music festival last year.

2 George ________ me that he had some new tracks for me to listen to.

3 I ________ everyone that I had a spare ticket for the concert.

4 Sally ________ that she couldn't go to the campsite because she didn't have a tent.

5 Laura ________ us to meet her in front of the stage.

6 I ________ I didn't know who the supporting act was.

3 ☆☆ Rewrite the reported speech as direct speech.

1 Ashraf said that he was in a café.
"I'm in a café. "

2 He told me that he was having lunch.
"________________"

3 He said he wanted to meet me.
"________________"

4 He said that he had been in the café for an hour.
"________________"

5 He told me he would leave in about 30 minutes.
"________________"

6 He told me to come quickly.
"________________"

4 ☆☆ Read the conversation. Then complete the reported speech below.

ME Hi, Dan!
DAN Hi! I'm really happy to see you! I have some exciting news. I'm thinking of going to a festival in the summer. I want you to come with me.
ME Hmm, I'm not sure. Where is it? How much is it?
DAN It's not far away. It's in the country. The tickets are about $30. I've been there before. I had a great time.
ME OK, but where would we stay?
DAN Well, there's a campsite. We can stay in a tent. It won't be expensive.
ME OK, I'll think about it.
DAN Great!

I went to the café to meet Dan.
He said that he [1] __was__ happy to see me and that he [2] ________ some exciting news. He told me that he [3] ________ of going to a festival in the summer, and then he told me that he [4] ________ me to go with him. I said that I [5] ________ sure, and I asked where the festival was and how much it was. Ashraf said that it [6] ________ far away, in the country, and the tickets [7] ________ about $30. He said that he [8] ________ there before and that he [9] ________ a great time. He also said that we [10] ________ in a tent, so it [11] ________ very expensive. I said that I [12] ________ about it.

5 ☆☆☆ Think of a conversation you had with someone recently. What did you talk about? Write at least five sentences using reported speech.

I was talking to Mom yesterday. She told me …

WRITING

An Email to a Friend

1 ★ **Read the email quickly. Circle the photo that matches it.**

a

b

c

Home Inbox Sent New

From: Karen To: Matt

Hello Matt,

[1]I just got your message, thanks. [2]It was nice of you to write!

You said you wanted to know all about the festival. I'd never been to anything like it before, but it was great! I only spent a day there, but I saw so many amazing things. There were a lot of people dressed as characters from movies and TV. I'm attaching a photo of some people I met. They live near you! They told me to say hello to you! I think I was the only one not wearing a costume! I felt strange walking around in normal clothes!

In the afternoon, there was an event with some really famous actors from *Star Wars*. There were probably around 500 people in the audience, asking questions. Unfortunately, I didn't get the chance to ask anything. But one of the guests said that she had just filmed something really exciting for the next movie. Then she told us! I can't say anything – it's a spoiler!

OK, [3]I have to go now. [4]I hope to hear from you soon.

[5]I'll be in touch later,

Karen

2 ★★ **Put a–e in the order they appear in the email (1–5).**

a [ ] request for a reply
b [ ] goodbye
c [ ] description of the festival
d [1] greeting
e [ ] thanks for writing

3 ★★ **Match the underlined phrases in the email (1–5) with the *Useful Language* phrases (a–e).**

a Write back soon. [4]
b Anyway, that's all from me. [ ]
c Bye for now. [ ]
d It was great to hear from you. [ ]
e Thanks for your email. [ ]

PLAN

4 ★★ **Write your own email about a festival you have been to. Take notes.**

What kind of festival was it? ____________

What did people wear? ____________

What did people do? ____________

What did you see and do? ____________

How did you feel? ____________

5 **Decide what information to include. Use the structure in Exercise 2 to help you.**

WRITE

6 ★★★ **Write your email. Remember to include the past perfect, reported speech, and phrases from the *Useful Language* box (see Student's Book, p89).**

CHECK

7 **Do you …**

- have a greeting and a goodbye?
- describe the festival?
- request a reply?

7 REVIEW

VOCABULARY

1 Match the definitions with the words in the box.

costume decoration fair fireworks float lantern parade program stall

1. something you use to make things look more interesting or beautiful ________
2. a plan of all the activities and events at a festival ________
3. a big table on the street where people can buy things ________
4. a big decorated truck that moves through the streets at festivals ________
5. a light that people can hold or hang up in public places ________
6. the clothes you wear for a special activity ________
7. something that makes beautiful lights and noises in the night sky ________
8. a large number of people walking together, usually to celebrate something ________
9. a place with games and machines you can ride on ________

2 Complete the sentences with words for live music and festivals.

1. There were three b________ m________ in Clean Bandit: Grace Chatto, and Jack and Luke Patterson.
2. At the end of the concert, the audience shouted for more, and the band came back for an e________ .
3. It was a terrible v________ for a concert. I couldn't see the stage because it was really far away.
4. I don't think this year's festival will be very good. The h________ is a band from the 1990s that no one has heard of.
5. We went to a small g________ last night – it was one of the best live events I've been to.
6. Did you know that there is a bonus t________ at the end of the album? Most people don't know about it.
7. Sometimes, the s________ a________ is better than the main performer.
8. The festival has a big c________ with space for nearly 500 tents.

GRAMMAR IN ACTION

3 Complete the sentences with the past perfect form of the verbs in the box.

be buy decorate hear not see sell

1. I didn't go to the festival because I ________ that it was going to rain.
2. I'm glad that we ________ the tickets early because they became really expensive later.
3. By the time the headliners appeared, the supporting acts ________ on stage for an hour.
4. My sister loved the concert. She ________ anything like it before.
5. When you checked the tickets online, ________ they ________ them all?
6. People ________ the street with lanterns and it looked beautiful.

4 What did Mike say? Change the direct speech into reported speech.

1 "I want to go home."
Mike said that ______________________.

2 "I don't feel well."
Mike said that ______________________.

3 "I've taken some medicine."
Mike said that ______________________.

4 "I'll take a taxi home."
Mike said that ______________________.

5 "I can't find a taxi number!"
Mike said that ______________________.

6 "I'll ask my mom to come get me."
Mike said that ______________________.

CUMULATIVE GRAMMAR

5 Complete the text with the missing words. Circle the correct options.

I live in a small town. It's nice, but nothing interesting ever [1]______. So I was really surprised when my dad [2]______ me that there would be a big celebration. He said that the bridge in the town [3]______ 200 years old this summer, and there would be a huge party. At first, I said that I wasn't interested. I [4]______ over that bridge thousands of times going to school and I [5]______ see it during my summer vacation. But then my dad said, "If you [6]______ to the festival, you'll have a great time." So I went. And it really was great! Everyone was dressed up in costumes, and they had a parade through the center of town. The whole town [7]______ like a big history lesson! And in the evening, there [8]______ a big fireworks display. Earlier that day, I [9]______ that the bridge was really important in history. It [10]______ by a famous architect. I [11]______ it was just a boring bridge! It was a great day, but I still don't think there are [12]______ in my town!

	a	b	c
1	happens	had happened	is happening
2	said	asked	told
3	is being	would be	should be
4	have been	had	was
5	not want	didn't want to	didn't wanted
6	come	will come	came
7	looks	looking	looked
8	was	were	had been
9	was learning	had learned	have learned
10	is built	built	was built
11	was thinking	used to think	don't think
12	festivals enough	too festivals	enough festivals

8 What is education?

VOCABULARY
School

1 ★ **Circle the correct verbs to complete the phrases about school.**

1 *cheat* / *pay* on a test
2 *tell* / *fail* an exam
3 *get* / *pay* detention
4 *study* / *get* good grades
5 *pay* / *give* (somebody) a talk
6 *hand* / *pass* in homework
7 *cheat* / *pass* an exam
8 *pay* / *get* attention to the teacher
9 *study* / *take* for a test
10 *take* / *pay* an exam
11 *write* / *study* an essay

2 ★ **Look at phrases 1–8 in Exercise 1. Write them in the correct column.**

Positive Things	Negative Things
	cheat on a test

3 ★★ **Complete the sentences with the correct form of phrases in Exercise 1.**

1 I *took an exam* last week, but I'm not sure how well I did.
2 If you ________ for bad behavior, you won't be able to go to basketball practice after school!
3 He doesn't always ________ on his schoolwork – last week he got a D on an essay.
4 Tania was very pleased when she ________ all her ________ – she got As in history and science!
5 I can't go out tonight. I need to ________ on capital cities, and I haven't learned them all yet.
6 I ________ on ancient history – I got an F! I need to take it again.
7 Why did the teacher ________ you ________? What did you do to make him angry?
8 Please try to ________ on time, Sam! That's the second time you've given it to me late this week!
9 Someone ________ in Ms. Clarke's class. They used their phone to look up the answers!
10 Unless you ________ and listen to everything he says, you won't know how to do the project.

4 ★★★ **Complete the sentences so they are true for you.**

1 If I saw someone cheating on a test, I would ________.
2 It's important for me to get good grades because ________.
3 The last time I failed an exam was ________.
4 One important exam I will take this year is ________.
5 I usually study for tests ________.

Explore It!

Guess the correct answer.

The highest school in the world is called Phumachangtang in the Himalayas.
The school is more than ... meters above sea level.

a 4,000 b 5,000 c 6,000

Find an interesting fact about education in your country. Write a question and send it to a classmate in an email, or ask them in the next class.

READING

A Report

1 What do you think is happening in the photo? Read the report and check your ideas.

____

SCHOOL'S OUT

More than a million people are homeschooled in the U.S.A. **Reasons** for homeschooling can include a child's special needs, **bullying**, or **a lack of** good school options in the area. We spoke to one "homeschooler," Andrew James, from Atlanta, Georgia, about his experiences of homeschooling.

"I started homeschooling three years ago – I'm 14 now. When I left elementary school, I went straight to homeschooling, so I've never been to middle school. My mom was also homeschooled, so she was **into** us having a similar education to hers. My parents believe that education is not just about getting good grades or taking exams – they think a **balanced** education, including practical skills, is also important.

My younger brother and I study at home with our parents for seven hours a day. Both our parents used to be teachers – so that helps! But having school at home doesn't mean there aren't any rules. We're not allowed to stay in bed all day, obviously, but we can also choose what we learn. Of course, we study normal subjects, but we also frequently go to libraries, museums, exhibitions, concerts, and sporting events as part of our education.

We can also do other things that maybe you can't do at an ordinary school. For example, each year my brother and I are allowed to plan a big trip to a place connected to something we are studying. My brother studies geology, so we went to Mount Vesuvius in Italy to learn about volcanoes. Next year, I want to go to Amsterdam to visit the house of Anne Frank because I'm learning about her famous **diary** in my history lessons.

It's not all vacations and day trips – we work really hard and study a lot! But I really love my home education. I wouldn't change it for anything!"

2 Match the words in bold in the report with the meanings.

1 having equal amounts of something *balanced*
2 a book with someone's thoughts and feelings ______
3 the causes of an event or situation ______
4 very interested in ______
5 not enough of something ______
6 when someone hurts or frightens someone else ______

3 Read the report again. Are the sentences *T* (true) or *F* (false)? Correct the false sentences.

1 Andrew has never attended an ordinary school.
F. He went to an ordinary elementary school.
2 Andrew started homeschooling because his mom didn't like his school.
______
3 His parents taught at schools before they homeschooled Andrew.
______
4 Andrew and his brother do some studying outside their home.
______
5 Their trips to other places are part of their education.
______
6 Andrew would like to go back to ordinary school in the future.
______

4 Think of two possible disadvantages of homeschooling.

______
______

GRAMMAR IN ACTION

Can/Can't

1 ★ **What do the sentences express? Write *permission*, *prohibition*, or *ability*.**

1 Marcus can't leave yet because he has detention. ______
2 You got a very good grade on your essay. Can I read it? ______
3 Sonia can play two instruments, and she's a great singer, too. ______

2 ★ **Circle the correct options.**

1 In my school, we (can) / *can't* learn Latin if we want.
2 My sister *can* / *can't* speak Italian, but she speaks German well.
3 Mrs. Evans says I *can* / *can't* leave until I've finished this exercise.
4 *Can* / *Can't* I borrow your dictionary, please?
5 We *can* / *can't* understand you when you speak clearly.
6 You *can* / *can't* stay in bed all day. It's bad for you.

To Be Allowed To

3 ★★ **Put the words in the correct order to make sentences. Then mark (✓) the sentences that are true for your school.**

1 school / at / wear / allowed / Students / aren't / jewelery / to ☐
Students aren't allowed to wear jewelery at school.
2 lunchtime / allowed / phones / We / at / use / to / are / our ☐
______
3 break time / soccer / play / Students / at / are / allowed / to ☐
______
4 shout / allowed / aren't / the / You / teachers / to / at ☐
______

4 ★★ **Write questions and short answers with the correct form of *to be allowed to*.**

1 you / cycle to school? (yes)
Are you allowed to cycle to school? Yes, I am.
2 your teachers / give detention? (yes)
______
3 students / wear any clothes they like? (no)
______
4 students / talk during exams? (no)
______
5 your best friend / sit next to you? (yes)
______
6 your parents / help with homework? (no)
______

5 ★★ **Complete the text with the missing words. Circle the correct options.**

I think it's hard to be the youngest in the family. My big sister [1] ______ to go to bed when she wants, but I [2] ______. On Fridays and Saturdays, I [3] ______ stay up later, but not as late as my sister. And my big brothers [4] ______ watch late shows on TV! But they [5] ______ to leave the house without helping our parents. They [6] ______ go to college by car, but I [7] ______ drive yet, so I cycle to school. All the people in my family [8] ______ give me a talk because I'm the youngest – it's so unfair!

	a	b	c
1	(a) is allowed	b are allowed	c can
2	a can	b 'm not	c isn't
3	a can't	b can	c 'm not allowed to
4	a can to	b is allowed to	c are allowed to
5	a aren't allowed	b can't	c not allowed
6	a can	b can't	c aren't allowed to
7	a 'm allowed to	b can	c can't
8	a are allowed to	b is allowed to	c aren't allowed to

VOCABULARY AND LISTENING

A Phone Call

1 ☆ **You will hear an exchange student in the Netherlands talking about what she likes about the country. Write two questions you'd like to ask.**

______

______

8.01 **2** ☆☆ **Listen to the phone call. Does it answer any of your questions in Exercise 1?**

______

8.01 **3** ☆☆ **Listen again and answer the questions.**

1 What is the subject of the phone call?
studying and living in another country

2 How long will Julia be in the Netherlands?
______

3 What's her favorite thing about life in the Netherlands?
______

4 Why are drivers from the Netherlands usually polite, according to Julia?
______

5 How did Julia travel to school this morning?
______

6 Which country does Julia compare with the Netherlands?
______

Attitude and Behavior

4 ☆ **Complete the words with the correct vowels (*a*, *e*, *i*, *o*, *u*).**

1 r*u*d*e*
2 c_r_f_l
3 _mm_t_r_
4 p_l_t_
5 m_t_r_
6 c_r_l_ss
7 _rg_n_z_d
8 d_s_b_d_ _nt
9 d_s_rg_n_z_d
10 w_ll-b_h_v_d

5 ☆☆ **Complete the sentences with the words in Exercise 4.**

1 Rohan is a very *well-behaved* student: the teachers never need to give him a talk.
2 Patricia is a very ______ child. She never says "please"!
3 Our teacher likes us to be ______ and keep our desks clean and neat.
4 Please be ______ when you cycle in the rain.
5 Don't be ______ – you should check your homework for mistakes before you hand it in.
6 Our parents teach us to be ______ and thank visitors for coming to the house.
7 Bella's pens and pencils are all over the floor. She's so ______ with her things!
8 My little cousin is very ______! My aunt's always giving him a talk, but he never listens.
9 Molly is nearly 16, but sometimes she is very ______ – like a little girl.
10 Paul is younger than his sister Molly, but he's much more ______ and sensible.

6 ☆☆ **Match sentences 1–5 with a–e.**

1 Jorge is so careless. [*c*]
2 He's usually very mature. [ ]
3 Jon's a disobedient boy at home. [ ]
4 Try to be more polite. [ ]
5 Miguel isn't disorganized. [ ]

a He hardly ever does anything that is immature.
b It's so rude not to say "thank you."
c He should try to be more careful.
d His schoolwork is always neat and organized.
e But he's well-behaved at school.

GRAMMAR IN ACTION

To Have To, Must, and To Need To

1 ☆ **Circle the correct options.**

1 You (need to) / *don't have to* / *must not* study for exams.
2 He *must* / *doesn't need to* / *doesn't have to* be better-behaved in class – he's very disobedient!
3 Students *don't have to* / *don't need to* / *must not* wear makeup. It's not allowed.
4 We *don't need to* / *have to* / *must not* ask if we don't understand the questions.
5 You *don't have to* / *must* / *have to* finish the essay right now. It's for next week.

2 ☆☆ **Put the words in the correct order to make the Exam FAQs.**

Home News FAQs Sign In Register

Exam FAQs

1 need / we / to / an optional question / answer / Do / ?
Do we need to answer an optional question?
2 have / we / Do / to / a pen / use / ?
____
3 do / What / first / need / to / we / do / ?
____
4 if / we / What / have / do / to / do / not sure / we're / ?
____
5 do / need / What / to / we / do / before / finish / we / ?
____
6 have / we / to / Do / the exam room / stay / in / ?
____

4 ☆☆ **Are the sentences about the school notices *T* (true) or *F* (false)? Correct the false sentences with (*don't*) *have to* or *must*(*not*). Sometimes there is more than one possible answer.**

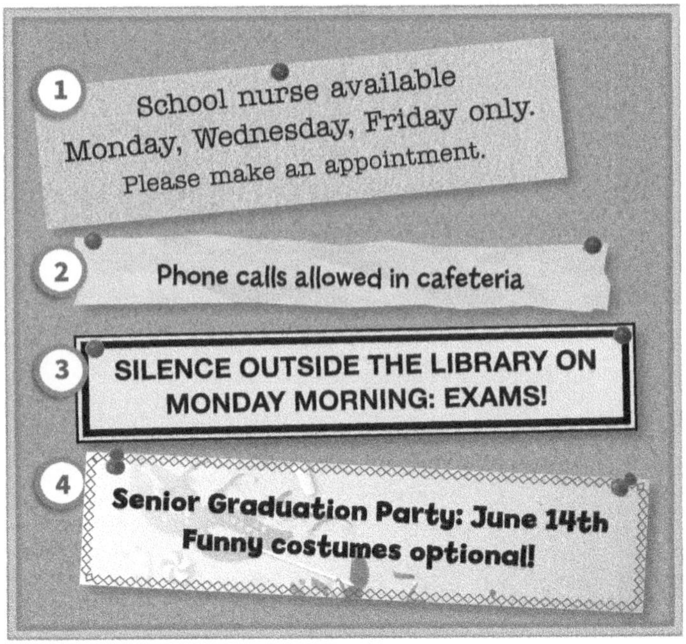

1 You don't have to make an appointment to see the nurse.
F. You have to / must make an appointment to see the nurse.
2 Students don't have to turn off their phones in the cafeteria.
____
3 You must not make noise outside the library on Monday morning.
____
4 Students must wear a funny costume to the graduation party.
____

3 ☆☆ **Complete the sentences with the phrases in the box. Then match the answers (a–f) with the FAQs (1–6) in Exercise 2.**

don't have to stay	don't need to answer	have to use	have to write	~~need to check~~	need to read

a You *need to check* all your answers before you finish. ☐
b You ________ in the room, but please leave quietly. ☐
c You ________ all the questions carefully before you answer. ☐
d If a question is optional, you ________ it. ☐
e Yes, you ________ a black pen. ☐
f You ________ something, so if you're not sure about an answer, don't leave it blank – guess! ☐

WRITING

An Essay

1 ☆ **Make a list of the advantages and disadvantages of digital technology in school education. Then read the essay. Does it have your ideas?**

____

____

Should We Reduce Digital Technology in the Classroom?

1 Most of us find it difficult to imagine schools without laptops or tablets, but some people believe that using electronic devices in class too much can be a bad thing. [1]essay. / In / outline / I / this some of the advantages and disadvantages of technology and give my own opinion.

2 [2]hand, / the / On / one using digital technology in the classroom can be more exciting than learning from books. Technology can also encourage more students to take part in group work through online activities. It is also believed that using technology can help students remember what they learn.

3 [3]other / On / the / hand, technology may cause students to stop paying attention in class. [4]that / Some / say technology is also bad for social skills, as students might speak to each other less during class. [5]argue / that / Others technology can make cheating easier for students – both in classwork and homework.

4 In my opinion, there are more important advantages than disadvantages, but there should be a balance between technology and traditional classroom work. Computers can never take the place of the teacher!

2 ☆ **Match the parts of the essay (a–d) with the correct paragraphs (1–4).**

a a conclusion with the writer's opinion 4

b bad things about digital technology ___

c an introduction to the topic ___

d good things about digital technology ___

3 ☆☆ **Put the underlined words in the essay in the correct order to make the *Useful Language* phrases.**

1 In this essay, I outline

2 ______________

3 ______________

4 ______________

5 ______________

PLAN

4 ☆☆ **Write your own essay. Look at the title and think of two good things and two bad things about weekend homework. Take notes.**

Is weekend homework a good or bad thing?

Good Things: ______________

____

Bad Things: ______________

____

5 **Decide what to include in each paragraph. Use the information in Exercise 2 to help you.**

WRITE

6 ☆☆☆ **Write your essay. Remember to include four paragraphs, *can/can't*, *to be allowed to*, *to have to*, *must*, *to need to*, and the phrases from the *Useful Language* box (see Student's Book, p101).**

CHECK

7 **Do you ...**

- have an introduction and conclusion?
- write about good things and bad things?

8 REVIEW

VOCABULARY

1 Match the beginnings of the sentences (1–6) with the ends (a–f).

1 The teacher will give you a talk if ☐
2 If you study hard for a test, ☐
3 It's always wrong ☐
4 If students don't pay attention, ☐
5 We usually have to write an essay ☐
6 If you study hard, you won't fail ☐

a when we take an English exam.
b the exam – you'll pass it.
c they won't know what to do.
d you'll get a good grade.
e to cheat on a test.
f you don't hand in homework on time.

2 Circle the correct words.

1 Jonty is very *well-behaved / disobedient*: he never gets detention.
2 It's *polite / rude* to talk when your teacher's talking.
3 I'm so *organized / disorganized* that I can never find anything.
4 She's only ten, but she's really *mature / immature* for her age.
5 *Careful / Careless* work doesn't usually get good grades.
6 You're so *well-behaved / disobedient*. You never do anything I tell you!
7 *Immature / Mature* people behave like someone a lot younger.
8 Be *careless / careful* with Ahmet – he's very sensitive!
9 He's very *rude / polite*: he always says "please" and "thank you."
10 Very *organized / disorganized* people plan everything they do.

GRAMMAR IN ACTION

3 Complete the sentences with *can*, *can't*, or the correct form of *to be allowed*.

1 In some countries, girls ________ go to school because their parents need their help.
2 Boys in that school ________ to wear long pants. They all wear shorts.
3 We ________ to have smartphones in the exam room. That's cheating.
4 You ________ use the library after lunch but not in the morning.
5 If you're late for an exam, you ________ to take it – you have to do it another day.
6 Your parents ________ help you because they don't know Latin.

4 **Complete the sentences with the words in the box.**

have to wear	have to worry	must run	must not run	need to come	need to meet

1 You really ________________ . The test starts soon.
2 We don't ________________ school uniforms on the weekend.
3 Sally doesn't ________________ . She's studied hard for the test.
4 My parents ________________ my teacher after school.
5 We ________________ in the hallways. It's dangerous.
6 Do I ________________ with you, or can you go alone?

CUMULATIVE GRAMMAR

5 **Complete the text with the missing words. Circle the correct options.**

HOME ABOUT ME ARCHIVE FOLLOW

Hello! In this week's blog I [1] _____ at exam preparation. Now, if you usually [2] _____ my blog, you'll know that I hate exams. I just [3] _____ do them! If I [4] _____ make exams disappear, I would do it! Anyway, I [5] _____ this subject a lot since my last post, and I think one important thing is planning: you [6] _____ start studying hard before your exams. You [7] _____ start months before, but at least a [8] _____ weeks. You [9] _____ also study at school as well as at home. Find a quiet place, like the library, so you [10] _____ concentrate. Little and often is the best way to study; an hour a day is great. Also, do exercise between study sessions – this helps you relax. I [11] _____ for a run in my local park. Finally, get a good night's sleep before the exam! For my last exam, I [12] _____ well the night before and I got a really bad grade. OK, that's all for now. More tips next week!

1 a look b 'm looking c had looked
2 a read b will read c have read
3 a can b can't to c can't
4 a could b can c would
5 a 'm studying b 've studied c 'd studied
6 a must b don't have to c must to
7 a have to b haven't to c don't have to
8 a few b little c enough
9 a shouldn't b should c should to
10 a need to b have to c 'll be able to
11 a 'm going often b go often c often go
12 a hadn't slept b haven't slept c wasn't sleeping

9 Where would you go?

VOCABULARY

Travel

1 ★★★ **Complete the puzzle. Use the clues.**

1 the place someone is traveling to
2 in or to a different country from yours
3 a family place with hotels, pools, and restaurants
4 when you travel somewhere and go back home in a short time
5 a large boat that you can go on vacation on (two words)
6 when you visit a place and look around it, often with a group of people
7 when you travel from one place to another, usually a long distance
8 a place to stay on vacation, e.g., a hotel, RV, or youth hostel
9 traveling with a large bag, usually visiting many places
10 visiting famous or interesting places on vacation
11 reserve a hotel room or a seat on a plane.

2 ★★★ **What are the hidden words in gray in the puzzle in Exercise 1?**

3 ★★★ **Complete the text with the correct form of words in Exercise 1. Sometimes more than one answer is possible.**

HOME DESTINATIONS FAQS

If you enjoy going [1] *abroad* and visiting exotic places, then Indonesia is one of the world's most interesting [2] __________. You can fly directly to the capital, Jakarta. Flights can be expensive, so it's best to [3] __________ early. You can also arrive by [4] __________, but this is a much longer [5] __________ by sea through Singapore or Australia. Jakarta is a lively city, and it's just a short [6] __________ by plane to the ancient city of Yogyakarta, where you can go [7] __________ and enjoy old buildings, temples, and even an active volcano. Many tourists go to the island of Bali, which offers many types of [8] __________, from expensive hotels to cheap hostels. You can, of course, stay in a large [9] __________, some with their own restaurants and private beaches. Finally, if you have a lot of time, Indonesia is a popular place to go [10] __________: you could spend months traveling around the country, enjoying the local food and culture.

Explore It!

Guess the correct answer.

A cruise ship creates the same amount of pollution in one day as ... cars.

a 5,000 b 20,000 c 1 million

Find another interesting fact about tourism and the environment. Write a question and send it to a classmate in an email, or ask them in the next class.

READING

A Magazine Interview

1 ☆ **Look at the photos of drones. Then read the interview and (circle) the best title.**

a The Dangers of Drones

b Why Drones Will Never Solve Transportation Problems

c How Drones Will Change the Way We Travel

2 ☆☆ **Match the words in bold with the definitions.**

1 staying away from someone or something *avoiding*

2 taking things like food or books to someone's house ________

3 working quickly and in an organized way ________

4 arrive on the ground after moving down through the air ________

5 not having a driver ________

6 big vehicles used to transport things ________

3 ☆☆ **Read the interview again. Complete it with the missing questions.**

Isn't this going to create a lot of problems?

Won't this make people lazy?

What other changes will there be?

~~How will we be traveling in the future?~~

What are the advantages?

4 ☆☆ **Read the interview again. Answer the questions.**

1 How will companies save money with new technology?

They will use driverless trucks.

2 Where might we see flying taxis soon?

____

3 What might be the biggest danger for flying taxis?

____

4 What three things make flying taxis better than normal taxis?

____

____

5 How will drones help people in danger?

____

Computer scientist Jeremy May answers our questions about the future of transportation.

1 *How will we be traveling in the future?*

I think **driverless** taxis will become common. Not only that, but companies will soon be using **trucks** that don't have a driver. This will save companies a lot of money. Some companies have developed a kind of flying taxi, too. It works like a helicopter, but it doesn't need a pilot – it's actually a drone. It's possible that some cities, like Dubai, will have a lot of flying taxis in the near future.

2 ________

Well, some people are worried that driverless taxis aren't safe. Flying taxis have to be even safer, of course. The skies are already full, so one challenge will be **avoiding** objects, like other drones, buildings, and birds. But most of us won't need to worry. It's likely that only the very rich will be able to travel by flying taxi – in the beginning anyway.

3 ________

First, these taxis will use electricity, so they will be more environmentally friendly. Second, they will be able to travel up to 180 kilometers per hour. This, plus the fact that they will be able to take off and **land** anywhere, means that they will be much more **efficient** than normal taxis.

4 ________

Companies will soon start **delivering** things by drone. In Dubai, a company tested a service for people who wanted a coffee but didn't want to travel to a café. The people just ordered online and got their coffee in a few minutes!

5 ________

It might! But the technology has a more serious use. We will be using drones to quickly send medicine or food to difficult-to-reach places like mountains and islands. This will be very useful in emergencies.

GRAMMAR IN ACTION

To Be Going To and Present Continuous for Future

1 ☆ **Complete the sentences with the phrases in the box. Then write *A* for the arrangements and *P* for the predictions.**

aren't going to find	is going to make		
~~'m going to~~	're traveling	's leaving	

1 Next week, I *'m going to* Spain on vacation. *A*
2 He ______ for the airport in an hour by taxi. ___
3 Technology ______ travel more environmentally friendly. ___
4 We ______ to Bali by plane, not cruise ship. ___
5 They ______ a way to travel that is 100 percent safe. ___

2 ☆☆ **Decide if the sentences are *A* (arrangements) or *P* (predictions). Then complete them with the best form of the verb in parentheses.**

1 I *'m meeting* (meet) Ed at four o'clock today. ___
2 She ______ (not enjoy) the cruise – she hates boats. ___
3 We ______ (go) camping in July. ___
4 They ______ (like) Madagascar next summer. The wildlife there is incredible! ___
5 Todd and Laura ______ (have) lunch at the airport tomorrow before their flight. ___

Future Continuous

3 ☆☆ **Put the words in order to make sentences in the future continuous. Then mark (✓) the sentences you agree with.**

1 abroad / in / I / 20 / living / be / years / will
I will be living abroad in 20 years. ☐
2 will / by 2035 / be / traveling / by flying taxi / Everyone
______ ☐
3 doing / all / Robots / jobs / in / will / be / ten years
______ ☐
4 50 years / living / other / won't / We / be / planets / on / in
______ ☐
5 using / won't / be / 15 years / gas / We / in / cars / in
______ ☐

4 ☆☆ **Circle the best options. For one answer, both options are possible.**

I read the other day that we [1]*are living* / *will be living* (circled) on Mars in the next 30 years. Well, you and I [2]*aren't going to live* / *aren't living* on Mars – they [3]*are only sending* / *are only going to send* their top astronauts in the near future! Normal people [4]*aren't living* / *won't be living* there for a long time. The famous scientist Professor Stephen Hawking said that we [5]*are going to need* / *are needing* to find a new planet in 100 years because we [6]*are having* / *are going to have* more problems with climate change and other things in the future. I [7]*'m giving* / *'m going to give* a presentation on space travel next week at school, so I've done some research! Hawking had previously said that in 1,000 years, people [8]*aren't living* / *won't be living* on the Earth at all. I'm not sure I agree – a lot of things can happen in 1,000 years!

5 ☆☆☆ **Write three predictions in the future continuous. Use the ideas in the box or your own ideas.**

communication	houses	music
relationships	work	

By 2050, people won't be communicating face-to-face anymore.
______
______
______
______

VOCABULARY AND LISTENING

Travel Phrasal Verbs

1 ☆ Complete the phrasal verbs in the sentences. Use the words in the box.

around	away (x2)	back	in	off (x2)	out

1 After we've checked __in__ to our hotel, I want to rest and then have some lunch.
2 We didn't go ______ this summer. We stayed at home for our vacation.
3 I always feel nervous when the plane is taking ______.
4 We have to check ______ of the hotel early – at nine o'clock – but we can leave our bags.
5 Out plane is at 2 p.m., so we need to set ______ for the airport at around 11 a.m.
6 I went to Guadalajara for a short business trip, but I didn't have time to look ______ the city.
7 It's nice to get ______ on vacation once a year and see a new place.
8 Our train was delayed, so we didn't get ______ home until late at night.
9 What time is your plane expected to get ______?

2 ☆☆ Complete the email with the correct form of phrasal verbs in Exercise 1.

Home Inbox Sent **New**

From: Marco To: Carmen

Hello Carmen,

I hope you're well! I'm really looking forward to your visit. What time does your plane [1] __get in__ on Tuesday? Let me know, and I'll [2] ______ early enough for the airport and pick you up. You won't need to take a taxi. I expect you'll be tired when you arrive, so I'll just let you [3] ______ to your hotel, and you can relax. You said you wanted to [4] ______ the city with my parents and me and maybe try some good local restaurants. Unfortunately, my parents are [5] ______ on business tomorrow. They won't be here when you arrive on Tuesday, but they're going to [6] ______ the day after. So why don't we all go to a nice restaurant later in the week?

Talk to you soon,

Marco

Conversations

3 ☆ You will hear two people planning a vacation. Look at the map and answer the questions.

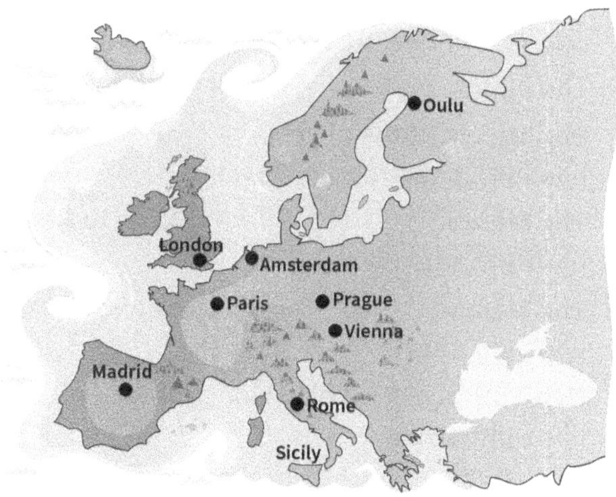

1 Which part of the world are they going to visit?
______
2 What's the best way to travel around and see all these places?
______
3 How much time do you think you would need?
______

9.01 **4 ☆ Listen to the conversation and check your answers to Exercise 3. Do Emma and Mason have the same ideas as you for questions 2 and 3?**

______

9.01 **5 ☆☆ Listen again. Are the sentences *T* (true) or *F* (false)?**

1 Emma and Mason can travel anywhere in Europe with their train tickets. __T__
2 Mason wants to go to the beach first. ___
3 Emma would like to visit museums. ___
4 Mason doesn't want to go to Finland because it's cold. ___
5 Mason would like to visit some European capitals. ___
6 Emma doesn't want to go to large cities. ___

GRAMMAR IN ACTION

Relative Pronouns and Relative Clauses

1 ★ Complete the sentences with relative pronouns.

1 The town *where* we went on vacation last year was very cheap.

2 The plane ________ I took was two hours late.

3 Spring is the time of year ________ you can see beautiful pink trees in Japan.

4 The reason ________ I want to go to Peru is to try the food.

5 The woman ________ suitcase was damaged was very upset.

6 New York is a good place for people ________ like sightseeing.

2 ★★ Correct one mistake in each sentence.

1 I remember the time where we went to London to see the Houses of Parliament.

I remember the time when we went to London to see the Houses of Parliament.

2 This is the resort I will be staying.

____

3 Is that the girl who bag got lost?

____

4 I lost the camera I brought it with me.

____

5 I have an app on my phone what tells me about all the best tourist attractions.

____

6 Mark is the person who I'm going to visit him in London.

____

3 ★★ Complete the text with the clauses in the box and the correct relative pronouns.

brings you	has traveled to lots of countries	I can see	I got a package in the mail	~~I want to visit Japan~~	opinion I trust

The reason [1] *why I want to visit Japan* is my brother Jonathan. He's someone [2] ________, including the U.S.A. and Australia, but he always says that Japan is his favorite place. He was working there when I was really young, and he often used to send me presents. I loved the moment [3] ________, and there was something inside, like a cool toy, food, or a *maneki-neko* (this is like a little cat [4] ________ good luck). So, Jonathan is the person [5] ________ the most about traveling to different countries – I always ask him for advice. I hope I can visit Tokyo one day and also other smaller towns [6] ________ traditional Japanese life.

4 ★★★ Join the sentences using a relative pronoun.

1 These are the people. I met them on vacation.

These are the people who I met on vacation.

2 France is the country. It has more tourists than any other country.

____

3 The departures lounge is a place in an airport. You wait for your plane there.

____

4 Drones are a new invention. They might replace normal taxis.

____

5 Norway is the place. I will be traveling there next summer.

____

6 Check-out is the time. We need to leave the hotel.

____

7 Linda is the person. Her brother is a pilot.

____

WRITING

An Email to a Host Family

1 ☆ **Read the email quickly. Mark (✓) the information that Bedour wants to find out.**

1 where Boston is ☐
2 what she will study in the course ☐
3 where she can find a place to stay ☐
4 when the course starts ☐
5 when the course finishes ☐
6 how to travel to Boston ☐

2 ☆ **Put a–e in the order they appear in Bedour's email (1–5).**

a ☐ goodbye
b ☐ questions about the trip
c [1] greeting
d ☐ reason for writing
e ☐ thanks

3 ☆☆ **Complete the email with the *Useful Language* phrases.**

a Best wishes
b ~~Dear~~
c Do you know
d I'm writing to
e thank you very much for

Home Inbox Sent New

From: bedour2004@mymail.com

Subject: Summer Course

[1] Dear Mr. Hamilton,

I hope you're well. [2] ________ check some details about my visit to Boston this summer. I'm looking forward to starting the course, and I hope I'm going to really improve my English!

As you may know, this is going to be my first time in the U.S.A. Is it possible to ask some questions? I received your welcome pack that gives information about accommodations. Unfortunately, the places that were listed all look a long way from the center of Boston. [3] ________ if I could find somewhere closer? I'd prefer not to spend too much time traveling each day.

I'd also like to ask about the exact dates of the course. I know the course will be starting on June 25, but do I have to arrive earlier? Could you also tell me when the course ends, exactly? I'm asking because it's important for me to book my flights.

Finally, [4] ________ accepting me into this course. My family is so happy for me!

[5] ________,

Bedour

PLAN

4 ☆☆ **Write your own email to a school abroad. First, decide what you are going to study and where. Write questions to ask your course organizer about these things.**

Your Travel Plans and When You Arrive:

____

____

Your Accommodation:

____

____

Your Course Content and Timetable:

____

____

5 **Decide what information to include. Use the information in Exercise 2 to help you.**

WRITE

6 ☆☆☆ **Write your email. Remember to include *to be going to*, the present continuous, the future continuous, and phrases from the *Useful Language* box (see Student's Book, p113).**

CHECK

7 **Do you ...**

- use a greeting at the beginning and say goodbye at the end?
- say why you are writing?
- say thank you?

9 REVIEW

VOCABULARY

1 Match the beginnings of the sentences (1–8) with the ends (a–h).

1 We arrived at our final ☐
2 I didn't stay in my own country for my last vacation; I went ☐
3 People like to visit the old market in my city – it's a popular ☐
4 I stayed in a big ☐
5 We went on several day ☐
6 I went online and ☐
7 If I had a lot of time, I'd like to ☐
8 Hotels, hostels, or villas: any ☐

a trips to local towns.
b abroad.
c accommodation is OK for me.
d resort, and my room looked out over the beach.
e destination on time.
f go backpacking across the country.
g tourist attraction.
h booked tickets for my trip next week.

2 Underline and correct six travel phrasal verbs in the sentences. Mark (✓) the correct sentences.

1 You need to check on at the airport two hours before your flight. ______
2 Please check in of the hotel right after breakfast, no later. ______
3 My plane gets in at five o'clock in the morning. I'm going to be so tired! ______
4 We're going out on vacation next week. Can you take care of our cat? ______
5 My dad is on a business trip right now, but he'll get away tonight. ______
6 I looked on the city, but everything was closed. ______
7 After the plane took out, I had an amazing view from the window. ______
8 What time are you setting off for the airport tomorrow morning? ______

GRAMMAR IN ACTION

3 Complete the sentences with the correct form of the verbs in the box. Use the tense in parentheses.

have	live	meet	not learn	study	visit

1 Next week, I ______ lunch with my grandparents. (present continuous)
2 This time next year, I hope I ______ science at college. (future continuous)
3 Some people think that we ______ on other planets in the future. (future continuous)
4 We ______ a lot of interesting places on vacation, I'm sure. (*to be going to*)
5 My host family ______ me at the airport at six o'clock. (present continuous)
6 Emma ______ much Spanish; she's only staying in Madrid for two weeks. (*to be going to*)

4 Write sentences using the correct relative pronoun from the options in parentheses.

1 The person was sitting near me on the plane is a famous actor! (who / whose)

____

2 I stayed at a resort is one of the best in the country. (why / that)

____

3 That's the passenger father is the pilot. (who / whose)

____

4 Cambodia is a country you can visit a lot of interesting old cities. (where / that)

____

5 The main reason I want to visit Italy is all the great food. (which / why)

____

6 June and July is a time there is a lot of rain in Japan. (when / where)

____

CUMULATIVE GRAMMAR

5 Complete the text with the missing words. Circle the correct options.

Usually, it only takes about 12 hours to fly from the UK to Thailand. That's not [1] ____, but so far it's been 32 hours [2] ____ I left home! I had set off for the airport early. I wanted to relax after checking in. After I [3] ____ in, the first thing I saw on the screens was that my flight [4] ____! At first, it was only two hours, then four, then eight! I [5] ____ that there were problems with the airplane. It [6] ____ in London yet. It was still in Moscow – about five hours away! The airline told me I [7] ____ stay in a hotel near the airport and they would pay for it. At 3 a.m., I [8] ____ a phone call saying that my plane had arrived, and that [9] ____ I went immediately to the airport, I would miss the flight! I got on the plane, and many hours later it landed at a new destination – Dhaka, the capital of Bangladesh! My plane needed [10] ____ some other passengers. I'm still in Dhaka now! [11] ____ here for four hours so far! I [12] ____ think that traveling was fun, but now I'm not so sure!

	a	b	c
1	long enough	enough long	too long
2	since	for	from
3	have checked	check	had checked
4	was delayed	delayed	is delayed
5	was told	was said	told
6	hasn't arrived	didn't arrive	hadn't arrived
7	can	could	would
8	get	got	was getting
9	if	when	unless
10	to pick up	picking up	pick up
11	I was	I've been	I'd been
12	used to	use to	did use to

EXAM TIPS: Reading Skills

Reading: Multiple Matching

You will read short descriptions of five people and match them with the best options. The options typically give information about places, services, entertainment, restaurants, etc.

There are eight options for five people, so there will be three extra. These extra options usually fit only partially.

Exam Guide: Multiple Matching

- To do this task, you should first read through the short description of each person. You should then decide what the most important information about each one is and underline it.
- Before reading through the options, think about what sort of thing you would recommend for each person. For example, if they like eating fish, you might recommend a restaurant that specializes in fish dishes.
- Then read through each option and underline the important information.
- Always double-check and read the information carefully. Are there any traps? For example, a young man might be looking for a summer job on an organic farm and one of the options offers this. But beware! The young man also says he wants to improve his **French** and the job is in **Spain**, so it is not the perfect match.
- Be careful not to "word spot." If the same word is in the description and in one of the options, it might be a trap and not a match.

REMEMBER!

Make sure the text you choose matches all the requirements in the person's description.

Reading Practice: Multiple Matching

Tip!

The descriptions and the texts often have the same information, but they are written using different words.

1 Read the text and match the words in bold with the words in the box.

accommodation	easygoing	famous	secretary
said we were sorry	said we would	star	talk show

I can really recommend the vacation [1]**apartment** in Pocos, where we spent two weeks. The owner is a TV [2]**celebrity** who has a popular late-night [3]**chat show** and is very [4]**well-known** in Brazil. We didn't meet her, but her [5]**assistant** was waiting for us when we arrived. We [6]**apologized** for being so late, but he was very friendly and [7]**not at all difficult**. We [8]**promised to** write a good review when we left!

1 ______ 4 ______ 7 ______

2 ______ 5 ______ 8 ______

3 ______ 6 ______

2 Look at the word in bold in each sentence and choose the option you think has the closest meaning.

1 That actor played the **lead** in a movie we went to see last week.
A director B hero C role

2 Parents shouldn't be too **harsh** with teenagers at exam time.
A strict B proud C miserable

3 This restaurant offers a wide **range** of vegetarian and vegan options.
A variety B line C sort

4 He works with a team of exciting and **innovative** young designers.
A athletic B creative C gentle

Tip!
Sometimes you have to guess the meaning of a word you don't know. Look at the context by reading the words and sentences that come before and after the word.

Tip!
Look out for traps! A useful way to check if your answer is correct is to think about why the other options are incorrect.

3 Read the descriptions of two people. Answer the questions.

A Gabriela wants to study English at a language school in Cambridge, where she has an aunt she can stay with. She loves soccer and wants to play on a team. Her language level is not very advanced, but she is very excited to learn. She wants small classes of mixed nationalities so that she has to speak English with her classmates.

B Winston is 25. He is very good at soccer and has played professionally. Now he wants to be a gym teacher, so he needs a teaching certificate in different sports. He is looking for a college outside a city with good sporting facilities and cheap college accommodation.

1 Which description mentions accommodation: A, B, or both?
2 Which description mentions student accommodation: A, B, or both?
3 Which person likes sports, especially soccer? Gabriela, Winston, or both?
4 Which person wants to teach sports? Gabriela, Winston, or both?

4 Read the descriptions of two colleges. Answer the questions.

Greystones College was built in 2003 in an attractive open area in the country just outside of Oxford. Places are available for our language-learning courses, which are taught in small numbers or intensively, one-on-one. Students stay with local families to give them the greatest opportunities to practice their language skills. There are good sporting and social activities all year round.

Hinton College is located in Cambridge, one of the UK's oldest and most beautiful university cities. The college has a a high level of success in English language learning. Our beginner classes are taught in groups of three or four by qualified native speakers. Social activities are arranged as part of the course, and team sports are encouraged. All of our courses are from one to six months in length.

1 Underline four important facts about each college:
- where they are
- what courses they offer
- how big the classes are
- what other activities they offer

2 What information tells you Greystones College is not suitable for Gabriela?
3 What information tells you Hinton College is suitable for Gabriela?

EXAM TIPS: Writing Skills

Writing: An Email

Writing an Email Response

For this question, you are given a short message from an English-speaking friend. You have to respond to the message in around 100 words. This tests your ability to understand a message and to write a clear response.

Exam Guide: Writing an Email

- Read the instructions carefully so that you understand who you are writing to and why you are writing.
- Your answer should be around 100 words. Don't write much more or much less than that.
- Begin and end your email correctly. Use:
  - your friend's name
  - an opening phrase.
  - one sentence for each point from the original email
  - a phrase to close
  - your name at the end.
- Start your sentences in different ways to make your email interesting.
- Don't copy too much language from the question. Try to think of synonyms where possible.

Writing Practice: Writing an Email

1 Read the instructions and the statements that follow. Are the statements true or false?

You are planning to visit your friend Robin in Canada. Read Robin's message. Then write an email to him.

From: Robin
Subject: Your trip!

Hi there!

I'm so happy to hear you are coming to visit me. You are going to love Canada!
On the first weekend you are here would you like to go ice-skating or to see a hockey game?
Let me know what kind of food you like to eat so we can buy it from the store. And don't forget to bring warm clothes. In January it's going to be freezing.

Can't wait to see you.

Bye!

Robin

	True	False
1 Your friend Robin is in Canada.	☐	☐
2 The message is from Robin.	☐	☐
3 Robin is planning to visit you.	☐	☐
4 You might go see a hockey game.	☐	☐
5 Robin has bought some food for you.	☐	☐
6 Your answer should be in email form.	☐	☐

2 **Read the sentences from two emails from the same boy. One is to his teacher, and the other to his friend. In your notebooks, write them in the correct order under the right heading, formal or informal.**

Formal	Informal

> **Tip!** Make sure you use the appropriate style: it should not be formal if you're writing to a friend.

I hope to be back at school on Monday.
I have a very bad cold and a high temperature.
Dear Mr. Jacobs,
Yours truly, Michael Fanshaw
Can you please send me this week's homework?
I apologize for my absence from class yesterday.

Bye, Mike
See you next week with any luck.
I have an awful cold – I'm coughing and sweating.
Hi Ana,
Let me know if there's any homework, OK?
Sorry I wasn't there yesterday.

3 **Change the words in bold to make the sentences more interesting. Use the words in the box or your own ideas.**

> **Tip!** Use a range of vocabulary: make sure you don't use the same word too many times.

amazing awesome boring colorful cool freezing great hate love pleasant prefer rainy

1 There's a **good** skate park with a **good** café near my home.

2 We had a **nice** camping vacation, but the weather was **not nice.**

3 I **like** swimming, but if you **don't like** it we can do something you'd **like more.**

4 The art galleries in my town are **not very interesting**, but the Museum of Tomorrow is **very interesting.**

5 We could go to the parade. It's very **nice** and the costumes are usually **nice.**

4 **Correct the mistake in each sentence.**

> **Tip!** Check your writing for any mistakes in spelling or grammar.

1 Don't forget turn off the lights when you leave.

2 Are you scared thunder and lightning?

3 The weather forecast says it's going snowing tonight.

4 I can't sing because I have a very hurt throat.

EXAM TIPS: Listening Skills

Listening: Multiple Choice

You will listen to short unrelated extracts and choose from three options. This tests your ability to listen for specific information and answer a question about what you hear.

Exam Guide: Three-Option Multiple Choice

- Use the time before you listen to read the questions. Read them carefully because they tell you what you need to listen for.
- All the possible answers may be in the recording, but only one will answer the question.
- Focus on the general meaning of what you hear. You may have to listen for the person's opinion, which is not necessarily a single word or phrase.
- If you're not sure, mark the answers you think are possible and check on the second listening.
- Always give an answer, even if you're still not sure. A guess might be right.
- Use the second listening to check, even if you're sure you're right. Don't stop listening!

REMEMBER!

You will hear the instructions on the recording. Listen carefully and read the question at the same time because this will help you understand the topic and the context.

Listening Practice: Multiple Choice

1 Underline two key words or phrases in each question.

1 What time does the girl's exam start?
2 What is the man going to buy?
3 Which evening activity is for beginners?
4 Why did Caroline leave her job?
5 Where are the teacher's keys?
6 What did Hari do this morning?

Tip! Underline the key words in the question. Then listen for the words that mean the same as the key words.

E.01 **2 You will hear a teenage girl speaking to her mother about an exam. Read the question below.**

What time does the girl's exam start?

A It starts at 11:30.
B Four o'clock.
C It begins at nine.

Now listen to the conversation. Why are options A and B not correct?

Tip! If the recording is a conversation, listen for the right person: who does the question refer to?

3 **You will hear two people talking about a play they've just seen. What words do you expect to hear in connection with the three options? Choose from the words in the box or use your own ideas.**

bad boring great impressive interesting old-fashioned too long too short

The Length	The Acting	The Costumes

E.02 **4** **Listen to the conversation and answer the questions.**

1 What did the woman think about the play?

A She thought the play was too long.

B She thought it was very disappointing.

C She liked the actors.

2 What did the man think of the costumes?

A He thought they were old-fashioned.

B He likes fifties fashion.

C He thought the clothes were terrible.

3 When is the play supposed to be set?

A the 1950s

B It's not mentioned.

C in the present

The First Conditional

If- Clause	Main Clause
(*if* + simple present)	[*will/won't, may/might* (*not*), *could*]
If I pass all my exams,	my parents will / may / might buy me a present.
If I don't pass all my exams,	I won't / may not / might not go on vacation.
Unless I pass all my exams,	
Main Clause	***If*- Clause**
[*will/won't, may/might* (*not*), *could*]	(*if* + simple present)
My parents will / may / might buy me a present	if I pass my exams.
My parents won't buy me a present	if I don't pass all my exams.
	unless I pass all my exams.
Questions	
Will my parents buy me a present	if I don't pass all my exams?

- We use **first conditional** sentences to talk about possible situations in the present or future and say what we think the result will be.
- We often use ***if*** + **simple present** to describe the possible action or event.
  We'll pass the exam if we work hard.
- We can use ***unless*** + **simple present** instead of *if not*.
  Unless we hurry up, we'll miss the train.
- We use ***will/won't*** + **infinitive** when we are sure of the result and ***may***, ***might*** or ***could*** + **infinitive** when we are less sure.
  If we don't leave now, we won't catch the 8:30 bus.
  If my grandfather doesn't feel better, he may not visit this weekend.
  I might go the beach if it's warm enough.
  If I'm lucky, I could win the race tomorrow.
- When we use ***if*** to start the sentence, we use a comma between the two parts.
  If I have enough money, I'll go on vacation.
- We normally use ***will*** to make first conditional questions. It is unusual to use ***may*** or ***might***.
  Will you chat with me online this evening if you have time?

The Second Conditional

If- Clause	Main Clause
(*if* + simple past)	(*would/could/might* + infinitive)
If I knew him,	I would / could / might ask him.
If I didn't know him,	I wouldn't / couldn't / might not ask him.
Main Clause	***If*- Clause**
(*would/could/might* + infinitive)	(*if* + simple past)
I would / could / might ask him	if I knew him.
I wouldn't / couldn't / might not ask him	if I didn't know him.
Questions	
Would you ask him	if you knew him?

- We use the **second conditional** to talk about imaginary situations in the present and their possible consequences.
- We use ***if*** + **simple past** (affirmative or negative) to describe the imaginary situation and ***would***, ***could***, or ***might*** for the consequence.
  If he didn't like you, he wouldn't talk to you.
- We use ***would*** (***not***) when we are sure of the consequence.
  He would do better in school if he didn't spend all his time playing computer games.
- We use ***could*** (***not***) to express a possibility or ability as a consequence.
  If it was Saturday, we could go out for pizza.
  I could do some volunteer work if I didn't need to study so much.
- We use ***might*** (***not***) to show we are less sure about the consequence.
  If I had more free time, I might take up the guitar.
  Madison might lend you her laptop if you asked her.
- We can use ***was*** or ***were*** in the ***if***- part of the sentence with *I*, *he*, *she*, and *it*.
  If it wasn't/weren't so spicy, I could finish it.
  I wouldn't say anything if I were/was you.

GRAMMAR PRACTICE

The First Conditional

1 Circle the correct option.

1 If I *have* / *will have* enough time, I'll help you pick up litter.

2 Unless Jenny calls, we *don't know* / *won't know* where she is.

3 Many more fish will die if they *eat* / *will eat* our plastic waste.

4 *If* / *Unless* we use solar power, we will reduce air pollution.

5 We might go swimming later if the sun *comes* / *will come* out.

2 Put the phrases in the correct order.

1 I might / I have enough money, / If / buy a new phone
If I have enough money, I might buy a new phone.

2 come to school later / you feel better / if / Will you / ?
____

3 if / Henry will / he leaves last / turn off the lights
____

4 climate change, / our planet / Unless / we stop / will get hotter
____

5 we'll miss / we don't leave soon, / the beginning of the movie / If
____

6 we collect all the plastic / The ocean / if / might get cleaner
____

The Second Conditional

3 Circle the correct option.

1 Our planet would be in danger if all the insects *would disappear* / *disappeared*.

2 What *would you do* / *did you do* if someone gave you a plastic straw?

3 Where *would you travel* / *would you traveled* if you had enough money?

4 There would be more oxygen if they *wouldn't destroy* / *didn't destroy* rainforests.

5 We could reduce the effects of climate change if we *would use* / *used* solar power.

4 Complete the second conditional sentences with the correct form of the words in parentheses.

1 If I had (have) the answer to the problems of climate change, I would tell (tell) you.

2 She __________ (not ask) you to come if she __________ (not like) you.

3 We __________ (not endanger) animals so much if we __________ (not destroy) their habitats.

4 If we __________ (live) near the ocean, I think our home __________ (be) in danger.

5 I __________ (not eat) meat if I __________ (be) you.

5 Underline and correct the mistake in each sentence.

1 What would you do if you had won a million dollars?
What would you do if you won a million dollars?

2 If you didn't work so hard, you would get so stressed.
____

3 Would those animals safer if they lived in a zoo?
____

4 I didn't eat fish unless I lived near the ocean.
____

6 Write second conditional sentences about the problems.

1 I don't have enough money to buy a new phone
have more money / buy a new phone
If I had more money, I would buy a new phone.

2 This coffee isn't sweet enough.
this coffee / be better / if / you add / a little sugar to it
____

3 We're not healthy because the air is polluted.
we all / be healthier / if / the air / not polluted
____

4 There are enough insects to feed everybody.
if / we all / eat insects / nobody / be hungry
____

GRAMMAR REFERENCE

Simple Present Passive

	Affirmative		Negative			
This bottle	is	made of plastic.	isn't		made of plastic.	
These toys	are		aren't			
Questions			**Short Answers**			
Is	this bottle	made of plastic?	Yes,	it is.	No,	it isn't.
Are	these toys			they are.		they aren't.

- We use the **passive** form to describe actions and processes when we are not interested in, or don't know, who is responsible for the action or process.
  English is spoken in many countries.
  Many plastic bottles aren't recycled.
- To form the **simple present passive**, we use ***is*/*are*** (***not***) + **past participle**.
  The streets are cleaned on Sundays after the market finishes.
- We form questions with ***Is*/*Are*** + **subject** + **past participle**.
  Is the main square decorated during the festival?
  When are the results sent to students?

Simple Past Passive

	Affirmative		Negative			
The trash	was	thrown away.	wasn't		thrown away.	
The old chairs	were		weren't			
Questions			**Short Answers**			
Was	the trash	thrown away?	Yes,	it was.	No,	it wasn't.
Were	the old chairs			they were.		they weren't.

- We use the **simple past passive** to describe actions and processes in the past.
  The contest winners were given books and a certificate.
- To form the **simple past passive**, we use ***was*/*were*** (***not***) + **past participle**.
  The first CD was made in 1982.
  Some of us weren't invited to the party.
- To form questions, we use ***was*/*were*** + **subject** + **past participle**.
  Were the instructions written in Spanish or Portuguese?

Passive + *By*

- We use ***by*** with the **passive** to show who or what was responsible for the action.
  The Merchant of Venice *was written by Shakespeare.*
  A lot of houses were destroyed by the fire.

GRAMMAR PRACTICE

UNIT 6

Simple Present Passive

1 Complete the conversation with the simple present passive form of the verbs in parentheses.

ANA How much waste [1] *is recycled* (recycle) in your home?

DAN Well, glass and metal [2] ________ (collect) every week. I'm not sure what [3] ________ (do) with the other materials we recycle. Some waste [4] ________ (burn).

ANA Yes, but burning waste isn't great. The air [5] ________ (pollute) because dangerous gases like methane [6] ________ (create).

DAN True, but you can do simple things to help. I never buy fruit that [7] ________ (pack) in plastic, and very little energy [8] ________ (waste) in our apartment.

2 Complete the text with the simple present passive form of the verbs in the box.

~~eat~~ fly not grow pack process produce sell send

A lot of the food that [1] *is eaten* in the UK [2] ________ there. Oranges, for example, [3] ________ in California. They [4] ________ there and then they [5] ________ to airports in Europe. Trucks transport the fruit to towns, where they [6] ________ in supermarkets. Incredibly, some food [7] ________ by ship to China, where it [8] ________ before returning to Europe.

3 Circle the correct option to complete the sentences.

1 Where ... ?
  a did BMW cars produce
  (b) are BMW cars produced
  c produced BMW cars by

2 The equipment ... in a small factory near here.
  a is pack b packed c is packed

3 A very strong tape ... these boxes.
  a is secured b secures c are secured

4 Their work ... every day by the managers.
  a inspects b is inspecting c is inspected

5 The end product ... for many different things.
  a uses b is used c has used

Simple Past Passive

4 Complete the sentences with the simple past passive form of the verbs in parentheses.

1 The Frisbee *was invented* (invent) by American college students.

2 The Shard ________ (build) near the river in London.

3 My favorite picture ________ (paint) by Frida Kahlo.

4 The factory workers ________ (not pay) very much.

5 English ________ (speak) in many of the resorts.

5 Write questions using the simple past passive.

1 what clothes / wear / by teenagers in the 1950s
  What clothes were worn by teenagers in the 1950s?

2 who / that amazing building / design by
  ____

3 where / the American soldiers / send
  ____

4 what / those old wooden boxes / use for
  ____

6 Answer the questions in Exercise 5. Use the information given.

1 blue jeans and T-shirts
  Blue jeans and T-shirts were worn by teenagers in the 1950s.

2 Frank Lloyd Wright
  ____

3 to Europe
  ____

4 packing equipment
  ____

7 Rewrite the questions using the simple past passive with *by* in your notebooks.

1 Who found those beautiful cave paintings?
  Who were those beautiful cave paintings found by?

2 What destroyed the city of Pompeii?

3 Who wrote *Romeo and Juliet*?

4 Who built Machu Picchu?

GRAMMAR REFERENCE UNIT 7

Past Perfect

Affirmative	
I / You / He / She / It / We / You / They	had forgotten.

Negative	
I / You / He / She / It / We / You / They	hadn't (had + not) forgotten.

Questions		
Had	I / you / he / she / it / we / you / they	forgotten?

Short Answers		
Yes,	I / you / he / she / it / we / you / they	had.
No,		hadn't.

- We use the **past perfect** with other past tenses to talk about actions or states that happened before the main past action or state.
  We hadn't seen the news, so we didn't know about the storms.
  I couldn't call you on Friday because I had left my phone at home.

Reported Statements

	Direct speech	Reported Speech
Simple Present	"I **want** some new jeans."	He said (that) he **wanted** some new jeans.
Present Continuous	"We**'re making** our own clothes."	He said (that) they **were making** their own clothes.
Simple Past	"I **had** a great time."	She said (that) she**'d had** a great time.
Present Perfect	"We**'ve just seen** a live concert."	She said (that) they**'d just seen** a live concert.

- When we report somebody's words, we often have to change the verb forms – see the chart above for how the verb forms change.
- We often need to change pronouns in reported speech.
  "You have to arrive before 7 p.m." – He said (that) we had to arrive before 7 p.m.

GRAMMAR PRACTICE

Past Perfect

1 Complete the sentences with the past perfect form of the verbs in parentheses.

1 I couldn't go to the performance because I ___had been___ (be) sick.

2 She ______ (not sleep) very well, so she felt tired all day.

3 I was happy because my team ______ (win).

4 We realized that we ______ (meet) once before.

5 He ______ (know) about the event for a long time.

2 Circle the correct option.

1 When we arrived, the party ....
a already was started.
b has already started.
(c) had already started.

2 I didn't want to see the movie until I ... the book.
a was read b had read c hadn't read

3 When we heard the noise, we knew something ....
a had happened. b happened. c happens.

4 They were so late that the performance ....
a has nearly finished.
b nearly had finished.
c had nearly finished.

5 Yolanda ran to the station, but the train ....
a had just leave.
b had just left.
c was just left.

Reported Statements

3 Circle the correct option.

1 They (*say*) / *tell* that it's the biggest fair in the world.

2 Edwin *said* / *told* everyone that he wasn't coming.

3 Did anyone *say* / *tell* you what time the movie started?

4 I have already *said* / *told* you not to do that.

5 The ticket *says* / *tells* that costumes are optional.

4 Write the direct speech in reported speech.

1 "I had an interesting vacation."
He said (that) ___he'd had an interesting vacation___.

2 "I've already read the movie review."
Maria said (that) ______.

3 "We're making pizzas for dinner."
They said (that) ______.

4 "Juan can't leave before eight."
I told them (that) ______.

5 Write the reported speech in direct speech.

1 She said she'd bought tickets for the exhibition.
"___I've bought tickets for the exhibition.___"

2 He told me he didn't watch any daytime TV.
"______"

3 Jacky said she was waiting for her friend to arrive.
"______"

4 We told them we had never heard that band.
"______"

6 Read the email. Then complete the reported speech below.

Home Inbox Sent **New**

Hi Diana,

Bernie and I are having an awesome time in Rio! We're staying near the Copacabana beach, so we've swum every day. The festival has been amazing. I've never seen so many fabulous costumes. We've loved every minute! Actually, we don't want to leave!

Love, Susie

I've just gotten an email from Susie, who's in Rio with Bernie. She said they [1] ___were having___ an awesome time. She said they [2] ______ near the Copacabana beach, so they [3] ______ every day. She wrote that the festival [4] ______ amazing. She said that she [5] ______ so many fabulous costumes. She told me that they [6] ______ every minute. Actually, they [7] ______ to leave!

To Be Allowed To

Affirmative / Negative		
I	'm / 'm not	allowed to run.
We / You / They	're / aren't	
He / She / It	's / isn't	

Questions			Short Answers
Am	I	allowed to run?	Yes, I am.
			No, I'm not.
Are	we / you / they		Yes, we / you / they are.
			No, we / you / they aren't.
Is	he / she / it		Yes, he / she / it is.
			No, he / she / it isn't.

- We use ***to be allowed to*** to say that we have permission to do something.
  We're allowed to use my aunt's laptop.
  You're not allowed to take this book out of the library.
- We often contract ***to be*** in negative sentences.
  They aren't allowed to have phones in class.
  He isn't allowed to go to the party.

Must / Must not

	Affirmative	Negative
I / He / She / It / We / You / They	must go.	must not go.

- We use ***must*** to say what we think it is necessary to do, to talk about obligation, and to give strong recommendations.
  I must start studying more.
  You must listen to this song. It's fantastic!
- We use ***must not*** to say what we think it is necessary not to do, to talk about prohibition, and to give strong advice against something.
  We must not forget to buy her a present.
  Tell them that they must not be late tomorrow.
- Questions with ***must*** are not very common as they sound very formal. We tend to use ***have to*** instead.
  Must I go to bed so early?
  Do I have to go to bed so early?
- ***Must*** is the same in all forms.
- We use an infinitive after ***must***.

To Need To

Affirmative / Negative	
I / We / You / They	need to work. / don't need to work.
He / She / It	needs to work. / doesn't need to work.

Questions		
Do	I / we / you / they	need to work?
Does	he / she / it	

Short Answers					
Yes,	I / we / you / they	do.	No,	I / we / you / they	don't.
	he / she / it	does.		he / she / it	doesn't.

- We use ***need to*** to say that there is an obligation to do something.
  I need to go home after class.
- We use ***don't need to*** to say there is no obligation to do something.
  I don't need to take the bus. I can walk.

To Have To

Affirmative / Negative	
I / We / You / They	have to learn / don't have to learn.
He / She / It	has to learn / doesn't have to learn.

Questions		
Do	I / we / you / they	have to learn?
Does	he / she / it	

Short Answers					
Yes,	I / we / you / they	do.	No,	I / we / you / they	don't.
	he / she / it	does.		he / she / it	doesn't.

- We use ***have to*** to say what it is necessary to do.
  You have to answer all the questions on the exam.
  He has to wear a uniform to school.
- We use ***don't have to*** to say that it is not necessary to do something, but that you can do it if you want.
  You don't have to help me with my homework.
  Elsie doesn't have to get up early tomorrow.
- Question words go at the beginning of the question.
  How much homework do you have to do every day?
  When do we have to make a decision?

GRAMMAR PRACTICE

UNIT 8

Can/Can't, To Be Allowed To

1 Write affirmative [+] or negative [–] sentences with *can* or *can't*.

1 Susanna / come with us tomorrow. [–]
Susanna can't come with us tomorrow.

2 we / write in our English books. [+]
______

3 James / use his brother's bike. [+]
______

4 they / play in a professional orchestra. [–]
______

2 Write sentences with *to be allowed to* and the verb in parentheses.

1 We *'re allowed to wear* (wear) boots in the winter.

2 Andrea ______ (have) her laptop in class.

3 Franklin ______ (not / drive) his father's car.

4 Children ______ (not / be) rude to their parents.

3 Make questions and short answers with *to be allowed to*.

1 your teachers / give detention / yes
Are your teachers allowed to give detention?
Yes, they are.

2 your little sister / wear makeup / no
______
______

3 they / use online dictionaries / yes
______
______

4 we / eat all these cupcakes / no
______
______

5 Carlos / play soccer with us / yes
______
______

To Have To, Must, and To Need To

4 Underline and correct the mistake in each sentence.

1 She don't have to sit at the front of the class.
She doesn't have to sit at the front of the class.

2 You have be well-behaved on the school bus.
______

3 Luis and his friend needs to finish their homework.
______

4 Must we to come into school on the weekend?
______

5 Circle the correct option.

1 It isn't necessary to write a thank-you letter.
(a) You don't have to write a letter.
b You must not write a letter.

2 I can go to the gym by bike.
a I need to take the bus.
b I don't need to take the bus.

3 It's important for me to study for exams.
a I don't need to study. b I must study.

4 We're not allowed to run in the hallways.
a We don't have to run, but we can.
b We must not run.

5 You must watch this video!
a I strongly recommend it.
b I don't think you'll like it.

6 Complete the swimming pool rules with the phrases in the box.

don't have to use	don't need to bring	have to have	have to wear	must remember	~~must not come~~	must not run	need to pay

You [1] *must not come* into the pool area in outdoor shoes. You [2] ______ rubber shoes around the pool. You [3] ______ attention on wet surfaces, and you [4] ______ at any time. There are lockers in the changing rooms, but you [5] ______ them. You [6] ______ your own towel because towels are provided. However, if you do use ours, you [7] ______ to leave them in the basket provided. Finally, swimmers under the age of ten [8] ______ an accompanying adult.

To Be Going To

Affirmative / Negative			Questions	
I	’m / ’m not	going to tell him.	Am I	going to tell him?
He / She / It	’s / isn’t		Is he / she / it	
We / You / They	’re / aren’t		Are we / you / they	

Short Answers			
Yes,	I am.	No,	I’m not.
	he / she / it is.		he / she / it isn’t.
	we / you / they are.		we / you / they aren’t.

- We use ***to be going to*** to talk about future actions we have decided to do.
  After we finish school, I’m going to travel to Australia.
  My grandparents are going to stay with us this summer.
- We use the appropriate present form of ***to be*** (***not***) + ***going*** + ***to*** + **verb**.
  I’m going to wear my new jeans and my red T-shirt.
  We’re not going to take the bus.
- We form questions with ***to be*** + **subject** + ***going*** + ***to*** + **verb**.
  When are you going to start studying for the exams?
  Is she going to get here before nine o’clock?

Present Continuous for Future

- We use the **present continuous** to talk about future arrangements when they have a fixed date.
  They’re getting married this summer.
  What are you doing this weekend? I’m going shopping with my parents.

Future Continuous

Affirmative / Negative		
I / You / He / She / It / We / You / They	will / won’t	be lying on the beach this time next week.
	may / may not	
	might / might not	

Questions			Short Answers
Will	I / you / he / she / it / we / you / they	be lying on the beach this time next week?	Yes, I / you / he / she / it / we / you / they will.
			No, I / you / he / she / it / we / you / they won’t.

- We can use the **future continuous** to talk about actions in progress at a point in time in the future.
  My sister will be living in Mexico next year.
  Next Saturday, we’ll be sitting on the beach.
- We use ***will***/***won’t*** when we feel sure about the action in progress, and ***may*** (***not***) / ***might*** (***not***) when we’re less sure.
  They’ll be answering questions online at 7 p.m.
  We might be having dinner at 9 p.m.

Relative Pronouns and Relative Clauses

- We use **relative clauses** to make the person, place, or thing we are talking about clear.
  My aunt has a friend who makes beautiful bags.
  This is the song that I told you about.
- We use **relative pronouns** at the beginning of relative clauses. We do not repeat the subject pronoun when the subject of the pronoun and following clause are the same.
  We know a lot of people who live in the village.
  NOT ~~*We know a lot of people who they live in the village.*~~
- We use ***who*** or ***that*** to talk about people.
  The man who/that lives next door works at night.
  She’s the scientist who’s/that’s moving to Antarctica next year.
- We use ***that*** to talk about things.
  I don’t like books that have sad endings.
  I want boots that I can wear all year.
- We use ***where*** to talk about places.
  That’s the office where my uncle works.
  Try the restaurant where we had my party.
- We use ***when*** to talk about time.
  That was the day when we were late for school.
  It’s the holiday when everyone is happiest.
- We use ***why*** to talk about reasons.
  You studied a lot. That’s the reason why you passed!
  I lost my passport. That’s the reason why I’m so sad.
- We use ***whose*** to talk about possessions.
  Do you remember the name of the guy whose phone charger I borrowed last week?

GRAMMAR PRACTICE

UNIT 9

To Be Going To

1 Complete the sentences with the correct form of *to be going to* and the verb in parentheses.

1 We ___are going to visit___ (visit) our old neighbors on the weekend.

2 She ______________ (not come) with us to Peru.

3 He ______________ (leave) for the station at nine.

4 They ______________ (deliver) the products by drone next year.

5 Flights ______________ (not be) cheaper in future, are they?

6 ______________ you ______________ (buy) the train tickets online?

Present Continuous for Future

2 Put the words in the correct order.

1 train / traveling / on / to / the / night / Madrid / We're

___We're traveling to Madrid on the night train.___

2 meeting / the / friends / their / They're / on / bus

____

3 on / summer / going / I'm / trip / this / school / a

____

4 for / you / Are / birthday / having / a / your / party / ?

____

5 tonight / isn't / our / Stella / to / concert / coming

____

Future Continuous

3 Complete the text with the phrases in the box.

will be building	will be cycling	~~will be driving~~
will be making	will be using	won't be doing

More people [1] ___will be driving___ electric cars in the future. Transportation companies [2] ______________ driverless trucks, too. But I wonder how teenagers [3] ______________ their daily trips in 20 years? Many believe that they [4] ______________ more, but they [5] ______________ that unless road conditions are improved. Today's cyclists hope that town planners [6] ______________ more bike lanes by the time their children are teenagers.

Relative Pronouns and Relative Clauses

4 (Circle) the correct option.

1 I didn't know the person (*who*) / *whose* sat next to me.

2 She's the girl *who* / *whose* mother is from Chile.

3 Is August the time *which* / *when* it rains a lot in Scotland?

4 This is the book *that* / *whose* was banned in the 1940s.

5 That's the place *why* / *where* they used to meet.

6 It's the summer and that's *where* / *why* I'm happy!

5 Underline and correct the mistake in each sentence.

1 Do you know <u>who</u> bags these are?

___Do you know whose bags these are?___

2 She can't remember when she wanted to buy.

____

3 That is the language school she will be studying.

____

4 I'll never forget the time why I met Adele.

____

5 Is there a reason where you don't want to fly?

____

6 Complete the conversation with the phrases in the box and the correct relative pronoun: *where*, *why*, *that*, *whose*, or *who*.

father was the artist	she recommended	told us
was the artist	we could wait	~~you took~~

ALEXIA Are those the photos [1] ___that you took___ on vacation?

KARL Yes, I took this one in Paris, remember?

ALEXIA Oh, I remember! We found a museum [2] ______________ for the rain to stop.

KARL That's right! This was the girl [3] ______________ about the exhibition.

ALEXIA I don't remember her. Was she the person [4] ______________?

KARL No, it wasn't her father, but she knew the man [5] ______________. That's the reason [6] ______________ the exhibition.

UNIT 5

Vocabulary

Planet Earth

carbon dioxide climate change
endangered species energy marine life
oxygen pollution solar power
the environment the planet waste wildlife

Natural Environments

bay cave cliff coast iceberg rainforest
stream valley volcano waterfall

Grammar in Action

The First Conditional
The Second Conditional

Speaking

Everyday English

I'll have to pass.
I'm off to …
It's not cool.
Wanna join us?

Useful Language

Don't forget that …
I see your point, but …
Let's agree to disagree.
Maybe you're right, but …
Remember that …

Writing

Useful Language

Writing an Opinion Essay

Furthermore, …
However, …
In addition, …
In my opinion, …
In my view, …
In summary, …
Some people believe that …

LANGUAGE BANK

UNIT 6

Vocabulary

Making Things

add boil cover dip freeze
increase place pour press pull
reduce remove stir

Materials

cardboard glass
leather rubber silk tin

Containers

bag box can
case jar tube

Grammar in Action

Simple Present Passive
Simple Past Passive

Speaking

Everyday English

any old …
Go for it!
Hang on a sec!
I get it.
kind of tricky

Useful Language

Giving Instructions

And there you have it!
First of all, …
Once (something is done), …
The next part's …

Following Instructions

Let me get this straight.
Oh, I see.
Then what?
What's next?

Writing

Useful Language

Writing a Review

The glasses look like …
The lenses are made from …
What I like about them is …
However, I should point out that …
Overall, I think it is / they are …

UNIT 7

Vocabulary

Festivals

atmosphere ceremony costume
crowd decoration fair fireworks float
lantern parade program stall

Music Festivals and Live Music

band member campsite encore
gig headliner stage supporting act
tent track venue

Grammar in Action

Past Perfect
Reported Statements

Speaking

Everyday English

at my place
Count me in.
It kicks off at …
I won't say a word.
The more the merrier.

Useful Language

I'd love to.
I'll be there (at/around) …
Should I bring anything?
What are you up to … ?
What time should I be there?

Writing

Useful Language

Writing an Email to a Friend

Anyway, that's all from me.
Bye for now,
It was great to hear from you!
Thanks for your email.
Write back soon!

UNIT 8

Vocabulary

School

cheat on a test fail an exam get detention get good grades give (somebody) a talk hand in homework pass an exam pay attention to the teacher study for a test take an exam write an essay

Attitude and Behavior

careful careless disobedient disorganized immature mature organized polite rude well-behaved

Grammar in Action

Can/Can't
To Be Allowed To
To Have To, *Must*, and *To Need To*

Speaking

Everyday English

How come?
Kind of.
That's no big deal.
Yeah, right!

Useful Language

Anything else I need to know?
What are the rules about … ?
What happens if you do?
Why's that?

Writing

Useful Language

Writing an Essay

In this essay, I outline …
On the one hand, …
On the other hand, …
Others argue that …
Some say that …

UNIT 9

Vocabulary

Travel

abroad accommodation backpacking book cruise ship destination journey resort sightseeing tour tourist attraction trip

Travel Phrasal Verbs

check in check out get away get back get in go away look around set off take off

Grammar in Action

To Be Going To and Present Continuous for Future
Future Continuous
Relative Pronouns and Relative Clauses

Speaking

Everyday English

… and so on.
bucket list
… right in the middle of …
the usual stuff
What were you saying?

Useful Language

How long are you going for?
I'm really looking forward to … (+ *-ing*)
… in two weeks
We're going to try …
What are you planning on doing?
Where will you be staying?

Writing

Useful Language

Writing an Email to a Host Family

Best wishes,
Dear Mr. and Mrs. …
Do you know … ?
I'm writing to …
Thank you very much for (+ *ing*)

IRREGULAR VERBS

Infinitive	Simple Past	Past Participle
be	was/were	been
beat	beat	beaten
become	became	become
begin	began	begun
bite	bit	bitten
blow	blew	blown
break	broke	broken
bring	brought	brought
build	built	built
buy	bought	bought
catch	caught	caught
choose	chose	chosen
come	came	come
cost	cost	cost
cut	cut	cut
do	did	done
draw	drew	drawn
drink	drank	drunk
drive	drove	driven
eat	ate	eaten
fall	fell	fallen
feel	felt	felt
fight	fought	fought
find	found	found
fly	flew	flown
forget	forgot	forgotten
get	got	gotten
give	gave	given
go	went	gone
grow	grew	grown
hang	hung	hung
have	had	had
hear	heard	heard
hide	hid	hidden
hit	hit	hit
hold	held	held
hurt	hurt	hurt
keep	kept	kept
know	knew	known
leave	left	left
lend	lent	lent

Infinitive	Simple Past	Past Participle
let	let	let
lie	lied	lied
light	lit	lit
lose	lost	lost
make	made	made
mean	meant	meant
meet	met	met
pay	paid	paid
put	put	put
read	read	read
ride	rode	ridden
ring	rang	rung
rise	rose	risen
run	ran	run
say	said	said
see	saw	seen
sell	sold	sold
send	sent	sent
shine	shone	shone
shoot	shot	shot
show	showed	shown
shut	shut	shut
sing	sang	sung
sit	sat	sat
sleep	slept	slept
speak	spoke	spoken
spend	spent	spent
stand	stood	stood
steal	stole	stolen
swim	swam	swum
take	took	taken
teach	taught	taught
tear	tore	torn
tell	told	told
think	thought	thought
throw	threw	thrown
understand	understood	understood
wake	woke	woken
wear	wore	worn
win	won	won
write	wrote	written

STUDENT'S BOOK ACKNOWLEDGEMENTS

The authors and publishers acknowledge the following sources of copyright material and are grateful for the permissions granted. While every effort has been made, it has not always been possible to identify the sources of all the material used, or to trace all copyright holders. If any omissions are brought to our notice, we will be happy to include the appropriate acknowledgements on reprinting and in the next update to the digital edition, as applicable.

Key: **CLIL** = Content and Language Integrated Learning, **F** = Finished, **U** = Unit, **VB** = Vocabulary Bank.

Text

U6: Text about Elif Bilgin. Courtesy of Elif Bilgin. Reproduced with kind permission of Abdullah Bilgin.

Photography

The following photographs are sourced from Getty Images:

U5: AROON PHUKEED/Moment; Jutta Kuss; John Holcroft/Ikon Images; s0ulsurfing - Jason Swain/Moment; Aolin Li/EyeEm; Yevgen Timashov/Cultura; Photographer who enjoys experimenting with various styles/Moment; MB Photography/Antarctica; sara_winter/iStock/Getty Images Plus; adiartana/iStock/Getty Images Plus; Wild Horizon/Universal Images Group; Peter Lewis/Oxford Scientific/Getty Images Plus; Puripat Lertpunyaroj/Moment; Ben Pruchnie/Getty Images; art-design-photography.com/Moment; Radius Images; VikramRaghuvanshi/iStock/Getty Images Plus; Hype Photography/DigitalVision; Timothy Allen/Barcroft Productions; goir/iStock/Getty Images Plus; CliqueImages/DigitalVision; Terje Eggum/AFP; Andrea Ricordi, Italy/Moment; **U6**: GOSPHOTODESIGN/iStock/Getty Images Plus; Spauln/E+; Ali Kabas/Corbis Documentary; Yann Song Tang/EyeEm; Milkos/iStock/Getty Images Plus; PhasuthornDesign/iStock/Getty Images Plus; hueberto/iStock/Getty Images Plus; puifaiminiiz/iStock/Getty Images Plus; happyfoto/iStock/Getty Images Plus; dmitriymoroz/iStock/Getty Images Plus; DonNichols/E+; Comstock Images/Stockbyte; aldomurillo/E+; novikat/iStock/Getty Images Plus; studiocasper/E+; DarrenMower/iStock/Getty Images Plus; by Chakarin Wattanamongkol/Moment; SasinParaksa/iStock/Getty Images Plus; carloscastilla/iStock/Getty Images Plus; Jerry Leer/iStock/Getty Images Plus; Delpixart/iStock/Getty Images Plus; **U7**: ferrantraite/E+; James Arthur Watulingas/EyeEm; Danita Delimont/Gallo Images/Getty Images Plus; Katsumi Murouchi/Moment; Emportes Jm/The Image Bank; Claudia Weirich/EyeEm; VisitBritain/Ben Selway; Thant Zaw Wai/Moment; Masumi Hamaguchi/EyeEm; Puay Ng/EyeEm; Elles Rijsdijk/EyeEm; Bill Heinsohn/Photographer's Choice/Getty Images Plus; bernardbodo/iStock/Getty Images Plus; watcharit praihirun/Moment; Rob Lewine; Marco Secchi/Getty Images News; © Philippe LEJEANVRE/Moment; Encyclopaedia Britannica/UIG/Getty Images Plus; Gareth Brown/Corbis/Getty Images Plus; Steve Debenport/E+; **U8**: Hill Street Studios/DigitalVision; Image Source/Photodisc; Glow Images; Neustockimages/E+; FatCamera/E+; Jose Luis Pelaez Inc/DigitalVision; AntonioGuillem/iStock/Getty Images Plus; PeopleImages/E+; Prasit photo/Moment; View Stock; Stockbyte; Chen Jie/The Beijing News/Visual China Group; MILATAS; Dexailo/iStock/Getty Images Plus; Paul Bradbury/OJO Images; Con Tanasiuk; Juice Images; monkeybusinessimages/Stock/Getty Images Plus; Sam Bloomberg-Rissman; Nutthaseth Vanchaichana/iStock/Getty Images Plus; Bulat Silvia/iStock/Getty Images Plus; **U9**: Colin Anderson Productions pty ltd/DigitalVision; Trinette Reed/Blend Images; Matteo Colombo/DigitalVision; sturti/E+; JodiJacobson/E+; brittak/E+; Chris Tobin/Photodisc; seb_ra/iStock/Getty Images Plus; Rtimages/iStock/Getty Images Plus; sorbetto/DigitalVision Vectors; Jochen Tack/arabianEye; RomoloTavani/iStock/Getty Images Plus; JIRAROJ PRADITCHAROENKUL/iStock/Getty Images Plus; PhotoAlto/Frederic Cirou; Ascent Xmedia/Taxi; Donald Iain Smith; Westend61; Jonathan Knowles/Corbis/Getty Images Plus; Photo by Scott Dunn/Moment; Rick Gomez; Morsa Images/DigitalVision; Kevin Boutwell/Moment; Kevin Arias Ceciliano/EyeEm; Matteo Colombo/DigitalVision/Getty Images Plus; adam smigielski/iStock/Getty Images Plus; ©Juan Carlos Vindas/Moment; Kevin Arias Ceciliano/EyeEm; jakkapan21/iStock/Getty Images Plus; Burak Karademir/Moment; Fgorgun/E+; Konstantin Trubavin/Indonesia; Jamie Grill; BrianAJackson/iStock/Getty Images Plus; kiszon pascal/Moment; Prykhodov/iStock/Getty Images Plus; Space-kraft/iStock/Getty Images Plus; mrtom-uk/iStock/Getty Images Plus; Pierre-Yves Babelon/Moment; Caiaimage/Sam Edwards; Monty Rakusen/Cultura; Haykal/United Kingdom; Oliver Rossi/The Image Bank; **U5—U9**: mocoo/iStock/Getty Images Plus; **F5**: JW LTD/Stone/Getty Images Plus; **F7**: Dimedrol68/iStock/Getty Images Plus; **F8**: Ben Pipe Photography/Cultura; **VB5**: Benjamin Wu/EyeEm; Feng Wei Photography/Moment; Fabian Krause/EyeEm; Arthur Machado/Moment; Eastcott Momatiuk/DigitalVision; Sergiusz Pawlowski/EyeEm; Ippei Naoi/Moment; Stephan Boehme/EyeEm; Antonio Zanghì/Moment; chain45154/Moment; **VB6**: Robert Kneschke/EyeEm; Kessirin Inta/EyeEm; 6381380/iStock/Getty Images Plus; dlerick/E+; Denise Torres/EyeEm; Saravut/iStock/Getty Images Plus; aopsan/iStock/Getty Images Plus; Fernando Trabanco Fotografía/Moment; Thomas-Soellner/iStock/Getty Images Plus; fotostok_pdv/iStock/Getty Images Plus; Salamatik/iStock/Getty Images Plus; kickstand/E+; **VB7**: Flashpop/DigitalVision; Hill Street Studios/DigitalVision; Zero Creatives/Cultura; Atlantide Phototravel/Corbis Documentary; Pirinal/iStock/Getty Images Plus; C. Colin Houck/EyeEm; Philip Gould/Corbis Documentary; LawrenceSawyer/E+; DigiPub/Moment; HuyThoai/iStock Editorial/Getty Images Plus; whitemay/E+; MarioGuti/iStock/Getty Images Plus; **VB8**: lisegagne/E+; Fuse/Corbis; Echo/Juice Images; Pixsooz/iStock/Getty Images Plus; Hero Images; AntonioGuillem/iStock/Getty Images Plus; Caiaimage/Martin Barraud; Tetra Images; Phil Boorman/Cultura; Fertnig/E+; Zulkhairi Dzulhasnan/iStock/Getty Images Plus; **VB9**: Konstantin Trubavin/Indonesia; **CLIL6**: Angelika/E+; Peter Von Walter/EyeEm; vlapaev/iStock/Getty Images Plus; **CLIL8**: Michele Falzone/DigitalVision; Nerthuz/iStock/Getty Images Plus; rudchenko/iStock/Getty Images Plus; andreknot/iStock/Getty Images Plus; Hero Images.

The following photographs are sourced from other libraries:

U5—U9: Carboxylase/Shutterstock.

U6: Courtesy of Elif Bilgin. Reproduced with kind permission of Abdullah Bilgin;

U8: Copyright © Christoph Otto.

Illustration

U5: Amber Day (Marie Bastille) ; Joanna Kerr; **U6**: Kay Coenen (Advocate Art); **F7**, **U7**, **CLIL8**: O. Flores.

Video Stills

The following stills are sourced from Getty Images:

U5: Scubazoo Images/Photolibrary Video; GeorgiaCourt/Creatas Video; GeorgiaCourt/Creatas Video; **U6**: RichVintage/Creatas Video; **U7**: phaitoons/Vetta; lavoview/Creatas Video+; **U8**: GeorgiaCourt/Vetta; Dalila Jocabed/EyeEm; Ascent Xmedia/The Image Bank; Yagi Studio/DigitalVision; **U9**: fStop/DigitalVision; stock-eye/Creatas Video; stock-eye/Creatas Video.

SU–U9: Lucentum Digital

Cover design and illustrations: Collaborate Agency

Typesetting: Aphik, S.A. de C.V.

Audio Recordings: Eastern Sky Studios

Video Production: Lucentum Digital

Contributing Authors: Liz Walter and Kate Woodford

Versioner: Suzanne Harris

American English Consultant: Multimodal Media

Freelance Editors: Mandie Drucker, Penny Nicholson, Cara Norris-Ramirez, and Rebecca Raynes

The authors and editors would like to thank all the teachers and consultants who have contributed to the development of the course, in particular:

Mexico: Ana Belem Duran; Nelly Marina Elizalde; Julio Andrés Franco Del Campo; Nimbe García Haro; Raoul Josset Paquette; Adriana Maldonado Torres; Ana Edith Ramos Ramírez

Brazil: Beatriz Affonso; Alessandra Bautista; Ana Carolina De Luca; Esdras Fattobene; Maria Claudia Ferreira; Itana Lins; Maria Helena Meyer; Valéria Moraes Novoa; Odinéia Morandi; Regina Pedroso De Araujo; Andrea Perina; Simone Rodrigues; Jacqueline Saback; Clice Sales; Silvia Teles

Turkey: Belgün Akçelik; Peggy Alptekin; Hayri Arslan; Ayşe Aylin Kündüroğlu; Nihan Çalışkan; Selin Dinçkal Erkenci; Bengü Özbek; Saliha Şimşek